TOUGH TIMES, GREAT TRAVELS

The **TRAVEL DETECTIVE's** Guide to **HIDDEN DEALS, UNADVERTISED BARGAINS,** and **Great Experiences**

New York Times **Best-Selling Author**
PETER GREENBERG
TRAVEL EDITOR FOR NBC'S *TODAY* SHOW

Sarika Chawla, Chief Research Editor

Rodale books may be purchased for business or promotional use or for
special sales. For information, please write to: Special Markets
Department, Rodale Inc., 733 Third Avenue, New York, NY 10017

Printed in the United States of America
Rodale Inc. makes every effort to use acid-free ♾, recycled paper ♲.

Book design by Christopher Rhoads

Library of Congress Cataloging-in-Publication Data
ISBN-10 1–60529–641–4 paperback
ISBN-13 978–1–60529–641–8 paperback

Distributed to the trade by Macmillan
2   4   6   8   10   9   7   5   3   1   paperback

We inspire and enable people to improve their lives and the world around them

For more of our products visit **rodalestore.com** or call 800-848-4735

CONTENTS

ACKNOWLEDGMENTS

I LEARNED A LONG TIME AGO that there are three kinds of people in the world: the people who make things happen, the people who watch what happened, and then there's the third category—one in which you don't ever want to find yourself—the people who *wonder* what happened.

But recently, we have watched as the people who *made* what happened suddenly began to *wonder* what happened, and as a result, many of us have found ourselves unwitting victims of a failing economy.

But are we really victims? Hardly. Within conflict and trouble lie opportunity. And, armed with the right information and resources, that upside remains almost unlimited.

That's the philosophy of this book, which was shared immediately by Karen Rinaldi at Rodale. And she, along with my agent Amy Rennert, championed the effort.

My chief research editor Sarika Chawla then assembled a great team of information sleuths, including Karen Elowitt, Dara Bramson, and Courtney Crowder, assisted by Michelle Castillo, Alix Proceviat, and Susannah Sachdeva, with additional help from Maria Lemus and Seda Terzyan.

We were able to assemble all the information in this book in record time—to make sure it could help many people as soon as possible. And that would not have happened without the tireless efforts of Meredith Quinn, who supervised the editing in New York.

Above all, I am especially grateful to Sarika for working virtually nonstop to meet an unforgiving deadline.

And now, the final result—a sort of guerilla travel guide to not just surviving the economic meltdown, but transcending it.

INTRODUCTION

WHEN THE GOING GETS TOUGH, the tough travel—that is, if they're smart. And the key to being and staying smart is having cutting-edge information immediately at your disposal so you can act quickly, even in the worst of times.

There was no adequate way to prepare for the economic crisis that still grips us. We're in the midst of a sea change affecting every level of retail, media, and information flow, not to mention the job market itself.

An initial reaction to that might have been to simply retreat into a bunker.

But as Dorothy told us in *The Wizard of Oz,* we're not in Kansas anymore. Even the folks in Kansas want to travel. Which brings me to the point: There's no upside to hiding in a bunker.

Right now, it's not important to travel just because we want or need to. It is, quite simply—and perhaps surprisingly—because we *can.* And we should.

And that's despite all of the bad economic news.

Personal bankruptcies, foreclosures, and liquidations are at all-time highs. Indeed, virtually every financial sign, every indicator, every projection, prognostication, and prediction has been gloomy, and with good reason.

A recent poll found that nearly half of all Americans plan to cut back on travel in 2009. Another survey found that at least 20 percent of us will travel less in '09. An American Express survey revealed—frighteningly—that 6 out of 10 people are worried about running out of money. In fact, there were those who argued that we woke up on New Year's Day to a $10 trillion hangover.

And that reflects the positive feelings!

Yet airline prices have not soared. In many cases, they've

dropped. The lodging industry is experiencing the strongest buyer's market in 33 years, with a dramatic power shift from seller to buyer. At the same time, as demand drops, supply is expected to increase between 2.5 and 2.7 percent this year and between 1.6 and 1.7 percent next year. That means hotel occupancy will dip below 60 percent, to its lowest level since 1971.

In the world of business and corporate travel, there's the concept of luxury shame coupled with "AIG syndrome."

What is AIG syndrome? That one's simple. No one wants to be seen getting a pedicure while Rome is burning.

The luxury market almost evaporated within hours of the news of the $400,000-plus tab American International Group senior management ran up at a Southern California beach resort after the insurance giant had received an $85 billion (and counting) bailout.

Now, after spending close to a decade trying to define the word *luxury* (or the new *luxury*), the panicked travel industry is scrambling to try to tell us what luxury *isn't*. It's an entirely new playing field for travelers looking for a deal.

And let's not forget what I call the "last supper" mentality.

I saw it in June 2008 when I flew to France on assignment for NBC. I landed in Paris at a time when the euro was topping $1.60, and I was prepared to see empty hotels and lots of restaurants with empty tables. Just the opposite occurred. Nearly every restaurant was full, and the hotels? Oversold. Booked solid by my fellow Americans, all of whom, it seemed, were crowded into hotel lobbies, standing around and complaining about how expensive it was to be there.

And when I talked to them, it was a revealing conversation. Surely, I said, you must have known what the exchange rate was *before* you flew across the Atlantic. Yes, they said. And yet, I countered, you traveled anyway. Why?

The answers—almost without exception—were similar and

disturbing. Well, we felt if we didn't come over now we wouldn't be able to afford it for the rest of our lives.

So there you have it. If you subscribe to that last-supper mentality, then the apocalypse is coming and, given the choice, when the going gets tough, the scared . . . travel impulsively. They whip out the credit cards, thinking that if they're going down, they might as well go down in flames. Paris, here we come!

Or Rome, or Madrid, or just about anywhere. The first signs of a failing economy didn't stop us from traveling. But what about a *failed* economy? Will that stop us?

In theory, if we travel on impulse, yes, it will. If we travel with intelligence and know our options and how to navigate the travel process, then no. But first we have to be clear with ourselves and then with others about when, why, and how we travel.

Six days after September 11, 2001, when the US airline fleet resumed flying, Americans were surveyed and asked if they were planning to travel. *No* was the overwhelming response. But those doing the survey forgot to ask a crucial follow-up question: Do you *want* to travel?

Of course we did. But we weren't sure we could. We needed someone to tell us it was okay to travel. We wanted our security blanket, and the travel industry did a poor job of providing it. So we didn't travel.

And now, the same first question is being asked, and the same first answer—*no*—is being given. But taking a closer look at the last-supper mentality as a social and psychographic indicator reveals that our desire to get out of town has actually intensified. Still, we need to know how to travel, how well we can do it, and how much it will cost us.

And therein lies the silver lining. Yes, there really is one. In the world of travel, 2008 was billed as the year of the *staycation*. I hate that term. It's a total fabrication, and it presumes that there is a long-term cause-and-effect relationship between the economy and our desire, our *need,* to travel. People still can fulfill that need to travel, and here's why.

In weakened economies, travel has fast become a major buyer's market. The dollar has suddenly gotten stronger. Entire countries are on sale: Mexico, Canada, South Africa, the Bahamas. Do you know what *kreppa* means in Icelandic? You will. It means *financial crisis.* Iceland has suddenly become half off. Korea is now a bargain, with the value of the US dollar rising almost 30 percent against the won. And the Australian dollar is trading at its lowest level in 5 years.

Everyone is discounting. Throughout the travel industry, however, especially at high-price-point hotels, not everyone wants to call it a discount. But travel—at all price points—is suddenly accessible to just about anyone and everyone.

The result of all of this: Even Disney World is discounting. Parts of the Caribbean are now ghost towns. Hawaii is operating at 50 percent tourist capacity. Ski resorts may be full of snow but are more or less empty of people. And what happens in Vegas can't stay in Vegas if no one is going to Vegas to make it happen to begin with.

And the cruise industry, hit with the double whammy of excess capacity and a worsening economy, is just about giving away cabins. During the final week of 2008, one Miami-based cruise line sold some cabins for—get this—$25.00 a night. And when I asked the chairman of that company how he was doing it, he sighed and said, "We're breaking even on good weeks."

News bulletin: These days, breaking even is the new black.

In the 30 years since deregulation, more than 142 airlines have permanently stopped flying in America. And that doesn't count the most recent mergers and consolidations. Our airports are congested; long flight delays are the norm, even in good weather.

The airlines are now charging fees for everything short of visits to the toilet and are calling it "à la carte" pricing. And even though the price of oil has come down, the fees continue to go up. Let me remind you that all of the à la carte pricing on airlines happened before the economic meltdown. Now, with the sad state of the US economy, it could get even worse.

At this writing, there are 574 airports in the United States that offer scheduled commercial airline service. By the middle of 2009, nearly a third of them will have either severely curtailed air service or will have no service at all. Airports in Cincinnati, Cleveland, and Columbus, Ohio; Houston, Texas; Las Vegas, Nevada; and Oakland, California, are expected to lose more than 10 percent of their scheduled service. Airlines are shrinking and cutting capacity—some by as much as 16 percent across the board. Right now, there are more than 500 aircraft parked in the desert, almost all of them permanently. That's the equivalent of taking one of the big-six airlines entirely out of service, which is devastating for the economies of cities and communities that now have limited air service, or none at all. And in the long run, it will be devastating for our national economy. The merger of Northwest and Delta into the world's biggest mega-airline is not giving a warm and fuzzy feeling to the city fathers of Cincinnati; Memphis, Tennessee; or Minneapolis, Minnesota.

Our entire air-travel infrastructure is at risk, and that, some argue, threatens our economy as much as—if not more than—the meltdown on Wall Street. Why? Without a robust, efficient airline and air-travel system, the economy sputters to a stop. Consider this sobering fact: Globally, airlines flew 46 million fewer seats in the last three months of 2008 versus the same period the year before.

And now, because of reduced capacity and fewer seats, every plane in the air is full. But, once again, there is a silver lining. We are at the intersection of price and opportunity: a depressed economy and the promise of great travel experiences. This is the new era of the contrarian traveler.

But the really important thing to remember as we watch bailout after bailout is not to get seduced by the seemingly convincing argument that a company—or an entire financial sector—is too big to fail. With the right ingredients and scenarios in place, everything—and anyone—can fail. So, in the travel industry, as we batten down the hatches and get into our bunkers to prepare for 2009, we need to remind ourselves of the power and impact of travel; of how it has consistently transcended events, demographics, and focus groups; of how it is at the core of our cultural DNA. Of how we *must* travel. So, it's not a question of whether we will travel, but how. And not how often we will travel, but how well.

What will determine that? First, refusing to board the panic train. Second, recognizing—and living—the essential distinction between the concept of being "too big to fail" and the more dangerous notion of being "too stupid to succeed."

When the going gets tough, the smart people travel. Tough times . . . great travels!

Check out **www.PeterGreenberg.com** for more travel tips, advice, and news you can use.

AIRLINES AND AIRFARES

IN 2007 AND 2008, there were 45 separate price hikes by airlines, with some fares rising as much as 40 percent.

And then came the summer and fall of 2008. Airlines cut flights, laid off thousands of workers, and, in the process of slashing capacity, slashed prices.

What's the best time to buy airline tickets? Wednesday morning (Tuesday night) when it's 12:01 a.m. in the time zone where the airline's hub is located.

Sound crazy? Here's how it works.

Airlines are still in the business of matching one another, so if one airline raises its fares (or adds a fee or eliminates a service or, these days, lowers its fares), the other airlines usually follow suit.

Airline fare wars usually start on Fridays. An airline announces a fare, a competitor counters with a lower fare, and, by the next day, all of their competitors match it. The going rate then drops more by Sunday night or Monday morning. By Monday night, another airline may jump in and offer an even lower fare to beat the competition, and by Tuesday morning . . . it's over.

Remember, once you book a ticket, you're given a 24-hour hold period to purchase it at that fare. By Tuesday at midnight, the airlines' computers cancel the orders of all the people who booked but didn't buy their tickets by Monday night, and suddenly all those low fares come flooding back into the system for a short period of time. And that's when you pounce. Wait any longer, and the cycle will start all over again on Friday.

Nickel-and-Diming Scheme 1:
Saturday-Night Stays

For years, airlines required travelers to stay over on a Saturday night to qualify for discounted airfares; the idea was to gouge business travelers, who tend to travel during the week. This practice pretty much disappeared with the rise of low-cost carriers, but with airlines scrambling to make money, the Saturday-night-stay requirement is back in several markets with American Airlines, Continental Airlines, Delta Air Lines, Northwest Airlines, and United Airlines.

Getting Around It

It sounds complicated, but for some travelers, back-to-back ticketing can save significant money. And there is a way to do it that won't piss off the airlines.

Say you have to fly from New York City to San Francisco for a business trip on Monday, April 6, through Thursday, April 9. No Saturday-night stay means you're going to pay through the nose, say $1,200.00.

So, you make that Monday, April 6, reservation from New York to San Francisco, but book the return for 3 weeks later. With the Saturday-night stay, your round-trip ticket will be significantly cheaper, say $400.00. Then you make a second round-trip booking, this time from San Francisco to New York on Thursday, April 9, and returning 2 weeks later.

If you plan it properly, you'll fly from New York to San Francisco using half of one booking and fly back using half of the other. Then you get another trip from New York to San Francisco and back using the remainders of the two round-trip tickets. That's two trips for $800.00 (and double the frequent-flier miles), as opposed to $1,200.00 for one.

Or just stick with budget carriers like Southwest Airlines, JetBlue Airways, Spirit Airlines, and AirTran Airways, which generally don't have Saturday-night-stay requirements and sell one-way tickets.

However, in what is perhaps a reflection of the times, things are changing. I recently looked into flying one-way from Los Angeles to New York. When I priced it on American—an airline that barely markets one-way fares—I was pleasantly shocked to discover that the one-way ticket was priced at an astonishingly low $149.00. And I pounced.

Budget Airlines

If handled properly, budget airlines can be your best friends. But if you don't follow the rules—well, just don't say I didn't warn you.

Budget airlines like JetBlue, Southwest, and Virgin Atlantic can be credited with lowering airfares across the board. There's even something called the Southwest Effect, a term that was actually coined by the US Department of Transportation to refer to the increase in air travel and drop in rates that took place whenever Southwest entered a new market. Bottom line: Increased competition means lower rates, and we have the budget airlines to thank for it.

Low-cost carriers are also an excellent way to get around cheaply in foreign countries. Traveling in Europe? Fly to London and then get to your destination city on a budget carrier. Two of the best known are Ryanair and EasyJet, but there are dozens of European budget airlines that proliferated in the early 1990s when airlines were first allowed to fly anywhere in the European Union without prior government approval.

Budget carriers have also made their mark in Australia and Asia, so if you can get yourself to a main hub, you have multiple options to choose from.

One big caveat: Travel light. If you show up at a no-frills airline carrying 60 pounds of luggage, you're going to pay for each and every pound over the minimum weight, and it adds up fast. Trust me on this one.

Find out which budget airline goes where at www.whichbudget.com.

Tip: Southwest doesn't release its data to travel search engines and aggregator sites like Kayak.com, Farechase.yahoo.com, and Sidestep.com, which means you can't compare it side by side with other airlines.

Secret Flights

Traveling from Vancouver, British Columbia, to New York City? Sure, you could fly Air Canada or United Airlines. But I bet you didn't know you could get there on the Hong Kong-based Cathay Pacific Airways—a leading airline that consistently wins awards for its service and comfort.

Welcome to the world of "secret flights": unusual routes flown by foreign airlines that you'd never guess would fly them. Are they really secret? No, they are published, scheduled flights with fares, but they aren't really marketed.

The airlines flying them use the routes as "fifth freedom" flights, meaning that individual countries have given these airlines the right to stop within their borders while en route to and from the airline's base country.

The benefit for you? You're on a nonstop flight that many people are not aware of, meaning fewer passengers and even lower prices—and, if you're on the right airline, much better service.

To fly from New York City to Frankfurt, you could travel nonstop on a United flight that's operated by Lufthansa, or you could travel on the award-winning **Singapore Airlines,** which stops in Frankfurt on its way to Singapore. Trust me, even in coach this airline beats United by a mile in terms of service, comfort, and food. And guess what? For every flight I compared, a round-trip flight on Singapore Airlines was either cheaper, the same price, or a maximum of $100.00 more than the United flight.

> **Tip:** If you really want to have some fun, log on to www.onetime.com. It finds fares on several travel search engines simultaneously and shows them in multiple windows on your computer.

Another of my favorite options is to fly nonstop from Los Angeles International Airport (LAX) to London's Heathrow Airport on **Air New Zealand.** A quick search on Kayak.com for a sample trip in May even showed that the Air New Zealand flight

Nickel-and-Diming Scheme 2: Unbundling

The term *unbundling*, or going à la carte, is just a fancy way of saying that airlines are now charging for everything short of using the bathroom in exchange for (theoretically) lower base fares.

Air Canada is a model for the unbundling system, giving you the option of choosing how many amenities you want included in the price of your ticket. This airline has four fare classes: The highest gets you a refundable ticket, priority check-in, food, and other amenities, while the lowest-priced option buys you only the seat along with the option to pay extra fees for upgrades such as food vouchers, advance seat selection, flight changes, and airport lounge access.

Some examples of unbundling:

• JetBlue charges $7.00 for a blanket-and-pillow kit on flights longer than 2 hours. And you know what? I'm okay with it. When you consider the state of most airline blankets (unwashed), $7.00 doesn't seem like a high price to pay for guaranteed cleanliness.

• Checking bags. See the Luggage chapter for more, but briefly, with American, Continental, Delta, Northwest, and United charging domestic economy passengers to check their first bag, we're now paying the airlines to lose our luggage! Continental even announced that the $15.00 fee to check that first bag is going to net the airline $100 million a year.

• Delta, Northwest, Virgin Atlantic, Virgin America, Air France, and Singapore Airlines now charge more for exit-row seats. It's a sure-fire way to get more legroom in coach, but at $15.00 to $71.00 each way, I'm not sure it's worth the extra 3 inches.

• US Airways now charges $2.00 for water, juice, and sodas; tea and coffee will cost you $1.00. I'm not a fan, but here's how you can get around it. The airline must provide free water if you need to take medication. So pick up a packet of M&Ms at the airport and explain to the flight attendant that you desperately need to take your medicine. Enjoy the free water.

was the cheapest option! It was at least $200.00 less expensive than flying nonstop on American Airlines, British Airways, Continental Airlines, Delta Air Lines, or any other carrier. Not only that, but you'll also get to sip New Zealand wines the whole way there, even in coach.

Then there are the flights from New York's JFK International Airport and Newark Liberty Airport on **Jet Airways,** which stop in Brussels, Belgium, en route to India. As a way to get to Europe, it's going to be a much better experience—on every level—than flying Delta from JFK or Continental from Newark. And, in most of the cases I checked out, the price on Jet was the same or less than that on Delta or Continental.

These secret flights usually show up on travel search engines like Orbitz.com and Expedia.com and on metasearch engines like Kayak.com and Mobissimo.com. Rule of thumb: If you see an airline listed that makes you go "Huh?" chances are, it's a secret flight.

Another handy Web site is Dohop.com, which tracks 660 airlines to tell you which ones fly your preferred route and at what approximate price.

You can also find out which airlines fly where by checking Official Airline Guide (OAG) at www.oag.com. Click on Airport Information and select the country, city, and airport to pull up a list of airlines that service it.

Flight Passes

If you're planning to travel extensively throughout a country or region, a flight pass may save you some cash.

The way this works is that instead of standard point-to-point tickets, flight passes allow you to take a limited number of flights within a given period for a flat rate. Flight passes are available from individual airlines, airline alliances, and travel brokers. Take a look at just a few examples of what's out there:

Air Canada has more than 25 passes, which are a series of one-way tickets that you pay for in advance. They cover almost all the destinations that Air Canada flies to in both North America and overseas. The passes usually include 4 to 10 credits (with each credit being valid for a one-way trip, including connecting flights) and are valid for 3 to 12 months, depending on the pass (some offer unlimited travel within a specific time period). Expect to pay between C$640.00 and C$14,000.00 (about $535.00 to $11,000.00) per pass, depending on the cabin class, the region, and the number of credits included.

▶▶ Air Canada, www.aircanada.com

Cathay Pacific's **All Asia Pass** not only gets you to Asia and back, it also lets you wander around 24 cities in nine countries. The pass includes round-trip economy-class travel between the gateway cities of Los Angeles, San Francisco, or New York and Hong Kong, then gives you the option of traveling to up to four other "basic" Asian destinations within a 21-day period. Rates for this pass start at $1,499.00 for flights to two destinations on Monday through Wednesday and go up from there to $2,099.00, not including add-ons.

▶▶ Cathay Pacific, www.cathaypacific.com

✎ Nickel-and-Diming Scheme 3: Fuel Surcharges

Airlines went into a flurry of adding fees and surcharges when fuel prices skyrocketed in 2008. That was all well and good when oil cost more than $140.00 a barrel. But the price dropped significantly by September 2008, and we are still paying a fuel surcharge. Why? Virgin Atlantic and British Airways finally dropped them in December, but other airlines haven't followed suit. Stay tuned on this one.

Malaysia Airlines offers the **Discover Malaysia Air Pass,** which allows you to take up to three flights anywhere in Malaysia (including the provinces on the island of Borneo) within 28 days for a cost starting at $199.00. However, the pass doesn't include the US-to-Malaysia flight, which you must purchase on Malaysia Airlines to qualify for the pass.

▶▶ Malaysia Airlines, www.malaysiaairlines.com

Qantas Airway's Aussie AirPass is very similar to the All Asia Pass in the sense that it gets you from the United States to Australia and also lets you visit several cities, all for one price. Prices start at $1,199.00 for a flight from Los Angeles, San Francisco, or Honolulu, plus three domestic flights within Australia. Prices go up from there, depending on the season and the zone you fly to.

▶▶ Qantas, www.qantas.com

Don't forget about airline alliances. Both **Oneworld** and **Star Alliance** offer multistop and round-the-world options, because you can pretty much fly anywhere in the world on partner airlines.

For example, **Oneworld's Visit Europe** pass lets you take as many one-way flight segments as you want to within Europe. The segments are priced at a flat rate according to distance, starting at about $85.00 per flight. For example, an itinerary involving London, Vienna, Budapest, Rome, Madrid, and Paris would only cost about €515.00 (about $740.00).

Oneworld's Visit South America option also charges a flat rate based on how many miles you're flying on partner airlines such as American Airlines, British Airways, and LAN Airlines (including LAN Chile and LAN Peru). Rates start at $102.00 for a short-haul flight of less than 350 miles and go up to $239.00 for up to 3,500 miles (getting to Easter Island will cost you more).

Star Alliance has 24 partner airlines compared with Oneworld's 10, which means more options—everything from Circle Asia Fare to Africa Airpass to an around-the-world plan. The price depends on how many stops you want to make.

▶▶ Oneworld, www.oneworld.com

▶▶ Star Alliance, www.staralliance.com

Top Airfare-Saving Sites

Airfare Watchdog: My friend George Hobica's site has real people scouring the Internet to find the best deals on the Web.

▶▶ www.airfarewatchdog.com

Yapta: Not only does Yapta track airfares, it also tells you if the price of a ticket you already purchased has dropped. If it has, Yapta will help you get a credit refund for the difference. It recently added a feature that alerts you if a seat opens up on a flight for which you can use your frequent-flier miles.

▶▶ www.yapta.com

Farecast: Don't know if you should buy a ticket now or wait until later? Plug in your route and Farecast will let you know if the price is expected to go up or down.

▶▶ www.farecast.live.com

Get Human: You can use this site to get in touch with hundreds of companies, not just airlines. It tells you how to bypass the automated phone system and talk to a live human being.

▶▶ www.gethuman.com

Fare Compare: Rick Seaney's site compares prices on more airlines than most other travel search engines (and even includes Southwest). It also maintains a database of airfares, which gives a historic perspective and helps predict future fare trends.

▶▶ www.farecompare.com

And, if you don't want to be locked into partner airlines, check out travel companies like **AirTreks** that get bulk discounts and travel agent rates. Live specialists can help you coordinate a series of one-way flights that won't force you to remortgage your house before you go.

▶▶ AirTreks, www.airtreks.com

Frequent-Flier Programs— Suddenly Redeemable Miles?

What do airline frequent-flier miles have to do with subprime mortgages and troubled banks? Answer: There are now more travelers with unredeemed miles chasing the available seats, and if frequent-flier programs were being run like the banks, they would all be in default on their "loans."

The economic crisis has inevitably focused new attention on the real meaning, utility, and overall worth of airline frequent-flier programs. And with good reason.

Of course, as travelers—or would-be travelers—we remain hopelessly addicted to mileage programs. And we'll do just about anything to get miles, even in a tough economy. A cartoon in the *New Yorker* said it all: It pictured a man pleading with the mugger who had just snatched his wallet, "Use the Platinum card. I need the miles."

And then there was the billboard promoting a loyalty program that featured a woman relaxing in an oceanside hammock at sunset. The copy read, "It's where hard-earned meets well-spent."

There's no argument that miles are hard-earned. But *well spent* presumes they can be redeemed *when* you want to redeem them, and that they can be redeemed at all.

Since American Airlines began its AAdvantage program in 1981, an estimated 124 million travelers have collected miles with more than 140 different airline mileage programs.

In fact, the most profitable division of any airline is its mileage program. That's right: It's how the airlines raise money. They print the currency and control the redemption. In fact, although the US Treasury is busy printing hundreds of billions of dollars for bailout programs, the airlines have them beat: They've been minting miles they *might* issue but that may never be redeemed and selling them to credit-card companies for advance funding. We're talking hundreds of millions of dollar's worth.

If you run the numbers, you could make the argument that United Airlines is a functional subsidiary of JPMorgan Chase, which is now its largest lender. And some of the banks in mileage programs are the very same ones that have advanced money to the airlines and therefore hold liens on their aircraft. That's the power of mileage.

In this era of financial bailouts, if we look at mileage as currency, then mileage is currently saving the airlines.

But can it also save you?

Even before the economy headed south, the airlines began devaluing your miles by the quarter, by the month, and sometimes by the week. Airlines are reducing the number of available seats and upping the minimum number of miles needed to get a seat.

In the process, airlines have forever changed the definition of "free flight." Consider the real cost of getting those miles. Most programs, which are usually linked to a high-interest affinity credit card, give you 1 mile for every dollar you spend. Because the minimum threshold to get a "free" domestic coach ticket is about 25,000 miles, you have essentially spent $25,000.00 to get that ticket.

So, let's do the math.

Let's say you used 25,000 miles (a.k.a. $25,000.00) to get a round-trip Los Angeles-to-New York City ticket, which in this environment averages $500.00. First, go to a site called Bankrate.com and calculate the interest charged on $25,000.00 worth of spending on your card; over a year, you would probably pay about $1,800.00 in interest alone. That $500.00 ticket just cost you $1,300.00! That simple calculation says it all.

Still, the programs are worth it—especially now—with a few important caveats.

How can you efficiently use the miles, especially in this economic environment?

For the moment, the key is not whether you can redeem those miles, but picking the best time to do it. And for my money (and my miles), the answer is a no-brainer. Do not wait. Do not stop. Do not pass go. Run, don't walk, and start to redeem those miles any way you can as fast as you can, and not just on your primary carrier, but also with its mileage partners.

But remember that these are no longer loyalty programs, they are marketing programs trying to change your purchasing habits.

So, the only real way to beat these programs is to never buy anything or change your buying patterns to get miles. That's the most absurd and wasteful approach to collecting miles. Only make a purchase you would have made anyway.

And then, do whatever you can to redeem those miles.

The good news: In this economy, there are suddenly thousands of unsold seats that airlines can make available for frequent-flier redemption. Right now, the greatest availability is on international flights, where airlines are wildly overscheduled for current demand.

So pick destinations you've always wanted to visit that have outrageously expensive airfares. And redeem your miles for those high-cost-ticket destinations. If you've collected your miles wisely, your miles will be used efficiently.

> **Bottom line:** Don't treat your miles as money. It's only a legitimate and truly valuable perk if you didn't spend any money over and above your ticket cost to get it.

CHAPTER 2

AIRPORTS

IF YOU WANT TO SAVE MONEY when you fly, you can't just pick an airline and a fare. You need a bigger financial vision—and it should include the actual route between points A and B. Some real money saving comes into play when you realize that the route is all about the airports involved.

Most and Least Expensive Airports

The US Department of Transportation's Bureau of Transportation Statistics releases lists of the major US airports that have the most expensive and cheapest average fares for domestic travelers to fly into or out of. Here they are, along with their average fares, for the second quarter of 2008.

The most expensive airports:

1. Cincinnati/Northern Kentucky International Airport (Hebron, Kentucky): $594.99
2. Greenville-Spartanburg International Airport (Greenville-Spartanburg, South Carolina): $568.25
3. McGhee Tyson Airport (Knoxville, Tennessee): $524.11
4. Dane County Regional Airport (Madison, Wisconsin): $468.37
5. Gerald R. Ford International Airport (Grand Rapids, Michigan): $461.23
6. Fresno Yosemite International Airport (Fresno, California): $460.48

7. Des Moines International Airport (Des Moines, Iowa): $454.40

8. Harrisburg International Airport (Harrisburg, Pennsylvania): $448.24

9. San Francisco International Airport (San Francisco, California): $439.34

10. Newark Liberty International Airport (Newark, New Jersey): $436.53

The cheapest airports

1. Dallas Love Field Airport (Dallas, Texas): $220.81

2. Bob Hope Airport (Burbank, California): $252.01

3. William P. Hobby Airport (Houston, Texas): $255.58

4. Chicago Midway International Airport (Chicago, Illinois): $256.73

5. Oakland International Airport (Oakland, California): $257.30

6. Long Island MacArthur Airport (Ronkonkoma, New York): $259.23

7. Orlando International Airport (Orlando, Florida): $262.63

8. Long Beach Airport (Long Beach, California): $263.13

9. McCarran International Airport (Las Vegas, Nevada): $266.34

10. Fort Lauderdale-Hollywood International Airport (Fort Lauderdale, Florida): $273.17

Notice something interesting here? Several of the most affordable airports in the United States are alternate airports.

What does that mean? An alternate airport is usually a smaller, secondary airport as opposed to a city's major international airport. Other times, there's a third, "secret" airport: Chicago's, for example, isn't even in Illinois. It's in Milwaukee, Wisconsin. Just look at the parking lot at General Mitchell International Airport and you'll quickly discover that a lot of Chicagoans have figured it out—more than a third of the cars there will have Illinois plates.

> Tip: Airport parking can really break the bank, so search around online for the lowest rates before you go. Check out national and international reservation sites like www.longtermparking.com, www.airportparkingreservations.com, and www.airportdiscountparking.com.

Alternate airports can translate into shorter lines, fewer crowds, and bigger savings. Here's why.

Budget Airlines Often Fly out of Smaller Airports

JetBlue services alternate airports such as William P. Hobby Airport in Houston, Texas (alternate to George Bush Intercontinental in Houston); Westchester County Airport in White Plains, New York (alternate to John F. Kennedy International and LaGuardia in New York City and Newark Liberty International in Newark, New Jersey); and Oakland International Airport (alternate to San Francisco International) and Long Beach Airport and Burbank's Bob Hope Airport (alternates to Los Angeles International) in California.

Southwest services Chicago Midway Airport (alternate to O'Hare International); Manchester Boston Regional Airport in Manchester, New Hampshire and T. F. Green International Airport in Providence, Rhode Island (alternates to Logan International in Boston); Bob Hope in Burbank and Ontario International in Ontario, California (alternates to Los Angeles International); Dallas Love Field Airport (alternate to Dallas-Fort Worth International); Bradley International Airport in Hartford, Connecticut (alternate to New York and Boston); Long Island MacArthur Airport in Ronkonkoma, New York (alternate to New York's JFK); and Oakland International Airport in Oakland and Mineta San Jose International Airport in San Jose, California (alternates to San Francisco International).

Spirit Airlines has a hub at Fort Lauderdale-Hollywood International Airport in Fort Lauderdale and also flies out of Palm Beach International in West Palm Beach (both alternatives to Miami).

And General Mitchell International Airport in Milwaukee is where you'll find **Midwest Airlines,** which services smaller airports such as Maryland's Baltimore/Washington International Thurgood Marshall and Bishop International in Flint, Michigan.

Many Smaller Airports Have Good Public Transit Links

Getting to Ronkonkoma's **Long Island MacArthur Airport** from Manhattan on public transportation is more of a hassle than taking the Airtrain to get to JFK, but it's definitely accessible. Colonial Transportation of Long Island offers $5.00 shuttle service from MacArthur to the Ronkonkoma Long Island Railroad (LIRR) train station, or you can take a bus between the two for $1.50. LIRR service to or from Manhattan's Penn Station will cost you $9.75 during nonpeak times and takes just under an hour and a half.

▶▶ www.macarthurairport.com

Palm Beach International Airport is in West Palm Beach, about an hour and a half from Miami, but you can take the Tri-Rail commuter train service directly from Miami International Airport in the center of the city to the Palm Beach airport for $5.50.

▶▶ www.pbia.org

Chicago's **Midway Airport** is one alternative to busy O'Hare, and it's actually closer to the city. About 10 miles from downtown, it is accessible via the Chicago Transit Authority's Orange Line for $2.00. Don't forget the previously mentioned **General Mitchell International Airport** in Milwaukee, which is an easy 90-minute, $22.00 train ride on Amtrak's Hiawatha Service. (As an added bonus, it's one of the most on-time Amtrak trains.)

▶▶ www.chicago-mdw.com

Getting to San Francisco from **Oakland International Airport** is simple on rider-friendly Bay Area Rapid Transit (BART). Just take the AirBART bus from the airport to the BART Coliseum/Oakland Airport station, where you can catch a BART train to any point in San Francisco. The whole trip won't cost you more than $4.00.

▶▶ www.flyoakland.com

Tip: Sleeping in an airport isn't an ideal way to spend a night, but think of how much you'll save. Some airports, like those in Vancouver, British Columbia, Canada; Dubai, United Arab Emirates; and Istanbul, Turkey, offer sleeping pods or by-the-hour airport hotels for naps. Or just check out SleepingInAirports.net, which shares travelers' experiences on the best and worst airports for snoozing. (The Golden Pillow Award consistently goes to Singapore's Changi Airport.)

And if you really want to plan ahead, bring along a Mini Motel. These portable tents fold to 17 x 12 x 3 inches and weigh less than 5 pounds. For about $50.00, you get the tent, an air mattress and pillow, a bedsheet, an alarm clock, a reading light, a toothbrush and toothpaste, earplugs, and an eyeshade!

▶▶ www.minimotel.net

In the Washington, DC, area, both **Dulles International** in Chantilly, Virginia, and Baltimore's **Baltimore/Washington International Thurgood Marshall (BWI)** are viable alternatives to Reagan National, and both are well served by low-cost carriers. Dulles, about 25 miles from DC, is connected to the Metrorail system by the Washington Flyer Coach, which departs about every half hour for the Metro West Falls Church Station and costs $10.00 for a 20-minute ride. Or you can hop on Metrobus Route 5A, which costs $3.10.

▶▶ www.metwashairports.com/dulles

From BWI, you can take the Express Metrobus to the Greenbelt Metro station, from which you can get to points in Washington, DC; Virginia; and Montgomery and Prince Georges

Counties in Maryland. The one-way bus ride will cost you $3.00 and takes about 30 minutes.

▶▶ www.bwiairport.com

An Alternate Airport May Be Closer to Your Destination than the Major Airport

Bob Hope Airport in Burbank, California, is about 3 miles from tourist attractions like Universal Studios and many of the television studios (for those free TV-show tapings!); Los Angeles International (LAX) is nearly 30 miles away.

▶▶ www.burbankairport.com

If you're headed to Disneyland, **John Wayne Airport** in Orange County or **Long Beach Airport** are going to be a better bet than LAX.

▶▶ www.ocair.com

▶▶ ww.longbeach.gov/airport

Traveling to Cape Cod, Massachusetts? You'll want to fly into Providence, Rhode Island, not Logan in Boston. The distance is about the same, but chances are that getting out of **T. F. Green International Airport** is going to be a much smoother experience.

▶▶ www.pvdairport.com

And **Dallas Love Field** is, well, in Dallas, unlike Dallas-Fort Worth International Airport, which is about 20 miles away.

▶▶ ww.dallas-lovefield.com

▽ Additional Resources:

Alternate airports, www.alternateairports.com
US DOT Bureau of Transportation Statistics, www.bts.gov
Hop Stop subway or bus directions, www.hopstop.com
Urban Rail, www.urbanrail.net

CHAPTER 3

AFFORDABLE ACCOMMODATIONS

SOMETHING TELLS ME you've been down this road before—probably many times: You find a great airfare and jump on it, but then you get nailed on hotel costs. After all, many destinations are inexpensive to get to, but outrageously expensive to be in. And if you're traveling overseas, the fluctuations in foreign currency values could easily put you in financial jeopardy.

People ask me all the time, "When is the best time to stay at a hotel?" And I've always given them what I thought was a logical answer: When everyone else isn't staying there. That means avoiding peak travel times like midweek in Manhattan, Super Bowl weekend in the host city, the Consumer Electronics Show week in Las Vegas, and other obvious periods. For resort hotels, you can more or less forget about the peak summer months between Memorial Day and Labor Day.

Want to know the best time of the week to book a hotel room? It's Sunday afternoon at around 4:00 p.m. local time. That's when revenue managers aren't working, and you can negotiate your rate with more flexibility. The trick is to call the hotel directly, not the central toll-free reservation number.

It also means taking advantage of opportunities when they're presented. And in some cases, that means after a major crisis. When New Orleans began rebuilding after Hurricane Katrina, newly reopened hotels were booking at rock-bottom rates. Deals appeared in the Caribbean during the long rebuilding process after Hurricanes Ivan in 2004 and Gustav in 2008, and in Mexico after Hurricane Wilma in 2005. Sure, you might have to put up with some closed businesses and noisy construction, but you can also expect great deals and hardly any crowds—it's a contrarian traveler's dream.

And then, of course, there are the "dead" weeks in the travel industry: the week immediately following Thanksgiving and the week after New Year's. During those 2 weeks, *no one* is traveling. They are simply recovering. You can just about go bowling in hotel hallways because no one's there.

But then Wall Street crashed in 2008 and, with the exception of the 2 dead weeks—which have become even more dead—there has been a change in the basic model of negotiating discount hotel bookings. In a desperate attempt to bring back visitors, travel deals have begun to emerge—and with few exceptions, they are *not* limited-time offers. Just about everything—everywhere—is now on sale.

After the crash, tourism in Hawaii dropped a devastating 20 percent from September 2007 to September 2008—and despite reduced air service, it's still expensive to get to Hawaii, but it's cheap to stay there as hotels and resorts have reduced their rates. Closer-to-home destinations like the Caribbean and Mexico have dropped hotel prices and thrown in airfare credit and perks like spa services and meals. Which brings us to:

The Silver Lining of an Economic Meltdown

In the unforgiving world of supply and demand, the economic meltdown has created a historic buyer's market for travel. And nowhere is this felt more than in the hotel business. Airlines have cut back on capacity, meaning that there are fewer available seats, and fewer people flying, which translates into thousands of unoccupied rooms and substantial discounts at hotels and resorts and on cruise ships.

The lesson here is that there's one silver lining to our economic meltdown: Travel deals abound. We're talking everything from free nights to air credit, free skiing, and rock-bottom "economic stimulus" rates.

And these resulting deals aren't just seasonal. By December 2008, hotels and resorts were advertising promotions that normally would have been applicable only during the first "dead week" after New Year's Day, but had been extended well into March and April. And in some cases, they were pushing those promotions through the end of 2009.

The catch was that most of these deals had to be booked by the end of December or January—basically, to ensure that hotels and resorts could fill their rooms through the spring. But deals are offered cyclically, and considering today's economy, it's likely that deals that would normally only be available in the slow post-Labor Day weeks will be pushed back into the summer months.

In order to get travelers back to the region, more than 20 hotels and resorts in **Los Cabos, Baja, Mexico,** banded together to create a promotion called Fly Me to the Sun. Through the end of 2009, guests checking out of participating establishments get a $400.00 refund on the final bill. For perspective, a night at the Westin Resort & Spa, one of the participating hotels, in late April starts at $275.00 per room, and airfare from Chicago to San Jose del Cabo for the same period can cost about $500.00, so the total cost of your vacation just dropped significantly.

▶▶ Fly Me to the Sun, www.visitloscabos.travel

Tip: I'm a big believer in consulting user-generated review sites to determine the quality of a hotel—as long as there is a vetting process and the number of users has reached a critical mass. At sites like Tripadvisor. com and Travelpost.com, even if a glowing "review" from a property's general manager sneaks through, there are enough legitimate reviews based on real experiences to give you an accurate picture.

In the Caribbean, one resort used the economic meltdown as a great marketing idea: the **Elite Island Resorts** Roll Back Your Stock's Value promotion. This Caribbean all-inclusive chain let visitors pay for a vacation worth up to $5,000.00 with stocks! Best of all, they assessed the stocks at their July 1, 2008, pre-meltdown values—so if you had 100 shares that were worth $40.00 each in July 2008 but $20.00 each when you booked, you got a $4,000.00 credit. Officially, to take advantage of this promotion you had to book by the end of January 2009 for a stay through December 20, 2009, but that was the official deadline. With just about everything being negotiable these days, the company may very well have extended the deadline.

▶▶ Elite Island Resorts, www.eliteislandresorts.com

Tamarijn Aruba now lets kids up to age 18 (two kids per two adults) stay for free all year-round—which adds up to significant savings when you consider that it's all-inclusive. We're talking all meals and drinks at 10 restaurants and 7 bars, nonmotorized water sports, rock climbing, a free kids' club for children ages 5 to 12, plus full use of the amenities at neighboring resort **Divi Aruba** (which also offers kids-stay-free promotions during certain periods of the year). Both resorts will also knock as much as 25 percent off the rate from early November to just before Christmas and in the hot summer months (don't worry, Aruba is outside of the hurricane belt). Let's do the math: A 4-night trip in late June for a family of four adds up to about $1,448.00—or about $90.50 per person per night, all-inclusive.

▶▶ Tamarijn Aruba, www.tamarijnaruba.com

▶▶ Divi Aruba, www.diviaruba.com

The all-inclusive **Franklyn D. Resort and Spa** in Runaway Bay, Jamaica, recently took 40 percent off of its regular rates through spring 2009. A family of four would normally pay about $3,500.00 for a 5-day stay in a one-bedroom suite, but with the discount it would cost $2,100.00, or $105.00 per person per night. And it's truly all-inclusive, which means the reduced price would include all of your meals, beverages (including alcohol!), and several activities, plus the added bonus of a free "vacation nanny" to play with the kids all day.

▶▶ Franklyn D. Resort and Spa, www.fdrholidays.com

Even luxury travelers are getting some perks. If you can shell out at least $2,000.00 a night to visit an all-inclusive private island, **Cayo Espanto** off the coast of Belize is offering free airfare. Through the spring, guests who stay a minimum of 5 nights in a one-bedroom villa get two free airline tickets or a maximum credit of $1,200.00. (Or go budget by staying in a smaller abode and get one free airline ticket or a maximum credit of $600.00.)

▶▶ Cayo Espanto, www.aprivateisland.com

Hawaii is capitalizing on its 50th year of statehood in 2009 with promotions to help lock in bookings. **Hilton Hawaiian Village Beach Resort & Spa**'s 50 Years of Aloha package is available until just before Christmas and includes 4 nights at $219.00 per night plus a 5th night at $50.00, and a $50.00 credit.

▶▶ Hilton Hawaiian Village Beach Resort & Spa, www.hiltonhawaiianvillage.com

Aqua Hotels & Resorts has dropped its rates through 2009 for a Nifty to Be Fifty Statehood Package that's available at 12 Waikiki properties that range from ultrabudget to boutique. You pay $50.00 for the 1st night of a minimum 3-night stay at any Aqua hotel in Waikiki, with additional nights costing $89.00 to $119.00.

▶▶ Aqua Hotels & Resorts, www.aquaresorts.com

Many deals and freebies can be found close to your own back-yard—no flying necessary. At the **Eldorado Hotel & Spa** in Santa Fe, New Mexico, a room costs $199.00 a night, but comes with a massage or facial for every night booked. When you consider that those treatments are worth about $130.00 apiece, you've practically recouped your losses in the form of spa treatments. It's not the worst way to go.

▶▶ Eldorado Hotel & Spa, www.eldoradohotel.com

Las Vegas is perhaps the most graphic example of the economic meltdown translating into incredible deals. Sin City is now Deal City.

The city already had too many hotel rooms before the melt-down, and airlines have cut capacity into Las Vegas by as much as 15 percent. This was the making of a perfect storm. In November 2008, the average daily hotel room rate dropped a staggering 28 percent. And at some hotels, rooms that were already discounted at $169.00 a night are now going for $59.00 a night. But it's not just room deals; there are a series of value-added offers as well.

The **Wynn** has recently reduced room rates, the **Riviera** is knocking 50 percent off in-room rates through July 2009, and The **Imperial Palace** has dropped its rates to just $33.00 on certain nights. That's just the beginning. Other hotels are offering free parking and airline credits.

▶▶ The Wynn Las Vegas, www.wynnlasvegas.com

▶▶ The Riviera Hotel & Casino, www.rivierahotel.com

▶▶ The Imperial Palace, www.imperialpalace.com

Ski resorts are doing whatever they can to get people out on the slopes. Normally, these deals would run only through January, but the resorts are now offering them through the end of ski season.

For example, at **British Columbia**'s **Whistler Blackcomb,** packages start at just $98.00 a night, and if you stay for 4 nights, you get the 4th day of skiing and the 5th night of lodging for free, along with free breakfast.

▶▶ Whistler Blackcomb, www.whistlerblackcomb.com

Even if you don't ski, the resorts are sweetening the deal. **Equinox Resort** in Vermont has an interesting package that starts at $999.00 per room for 3 nights and includes $999.00 worth of spa treatments.

▶▶ Equinox Resort, www.equinoxresort.com

And remember, this is the time to negotiate: Even if a deal isn't advertised, ask if your hotel or resort can throw in a ski lift pass, an extra night, or whatever it takes to get your business during the slower season.

Then there are the destinations you never even thought about visiting that have become affordable. **Iceland**'s currency has crashed so hard that now practically everything is half its normal cost—and the country is capitalizing on it. Various promotions such as the Winter Wellness Getaway from **Iceland Air** includes 4 days and 3 nights with airfare (from Boston's Logan or New York's JFK to Reykjavik) and a stay at a four-star hotel with spa treatments. Prices start at $699.00. (For comparison, last year just staying at the hotel for 3 nights would have cost you that much.)

▶▶ Iceland Air, www.icelandair.us

Affordable Stays

Saving on hotel costs doesn't have to mean hitting up friends of friends or sleeping in bunk beds with backpackers. You just have to be willing to think outside of the box.

Monasteries

Save money by sleeping with monks? Not quite, but monasteries and convents can be extremely cost-effective places to spend a night and get a (vegetarian) meal. You just have to be willing to follow the rules, which may include quiet or silent periods and curfews, and put up with spartan accommodations such as shared bathrooms and, in some cases, no double beds! Religious accommodations are prevalent throughout Italy, Spain, France, and England, but are also popular in parts of Eastern Europe, Asia, and—surprise—right here in the United States.

Just how cheap are we talking? **Istituto Maria Santissima Bambina** in Vatican City starts at around $65.00 per person for a double room. **Rila Monastery,** outside of Sofia, Bulgaria, can cost as little as $15.00 a night, but has become such a tourist attraction that rooms can book up weeks in advance. **Mount Saviour Monastery** near Elmira, New York, costs a suggested $45.00 a night.

Some monasteries are so devout that they don't charge visitors more than a few token dollars, but because they tend to cater to pilgrims, not just budget travelers, you may be required to attend prayer services and follow the rules to the letter.

Booking a room at a monastery or convent isn't always easy to plan. **The Church of Santa Susanna** offers a helpful listing of convent accommodations in the Rome and Vatican City areas. **Monastery Stays** is a booking service with comprehensive listings of Italian monasteries and convents. Other religious orders tend to have a limited Web presence, but there are several guidebooks and directories of monastic and convent guesthouses. If you can't call, fax, or e-mail in advance, check in with the country's or city's tourism board, or with specific religious orders, to help set up your stay.

▶▶ Istituto Maria Santissima Bambina, 39-06-6989-3511

▶▶ Rila Monastery, www.bulgarianmonastery.com/rila_monastery.html

▶▶ Mount Saviour Monastery, www.msaviour.org

▶▶ The Church of Santa Susanna, www.santasusanna.org

▶▶ Monastery Stays, www.monasterystays.com

Capsule Hotels

Capsule or "pod" hotels are still something of a Japanese phenomenon, but the concept behind these compact, affordable rooms is catching on elsewhere. The idea came from Japanese businessmen who often missed the last train home and would stay in rooms as small as 3 by 3 by 7 feet with nothing more than a bed and perhaps a wall-mounted television. Larger-scale capsule hotels—more often than not with private bathrooms—now exist in a few major cities, and often start at as little as $50.00 a night. This works if you only need a place to sleep and shower—and aren't prone to claustrophobia.

EasyHotel, owned by the same people who operate the budget airline EasyJet, currently has locations in London and Luton, England, and cities in Switzerland, Cyprus, and Hungary. Starting at around $57.00 a night, you get a room as tiny as 65 square feet, plus a cubicle bathroom. Like the airline, every amenity will cost you extra—from a couple of dollars to have your linens changed to a whopping £5 (about $7.00 a day) to watch the flat-screen TV in your room (you have to pick up a remote control at the front desk).

▶▶ EasyHotel, easyhotel.com

The **Qbic Hotel** chain promotes itself as being "cheap, chic and no frills," and rooms start at $97.00 a night. With properties in Amsterdam and Maastricht in the Netherlands and Antwerp, Belgium, these futuristic 70-foot-square rooms (a.k.a. Cubis) were designed by Feran Thomassen and Paul Rinkens and feature en suite bathrooms, Wi-Fi, and LCD televisions. The earlier you book, the cheaper the room.

▶▶ Qbic Hotel, www.qbichotels.com

What about Hotel Frequent-Stay Programs?

For once, all those points you've been earning for staying at major hotel brands can pay off. Blackout periods are being removed, and in general, fewer people traveling means there is now room available at the inns. This is definitely the time to burn those points—especially at expensive overseas hotels and resorts where availability has never been great. Timing, as they say, is everything. For domestic hotels, the rates are so attractive that you might want to hold on to your points and pay instead. The key is that rooms are vacant, so if you have points to spare, now is the time to take advantage.

The Art of Bartering

The art of bartering isn't dead, it's just taken on a new form. From trading nights on couches to weeks in entire homes, travelers now rely on the Internet to find one of the best deals out there: staying for free.

CouchSurfing and GlobalFreeloaders are two tried-and-true services that allow travelers to find a spare couch or guest bed. Though the average user age is about 25, couch surfing or swapping has become a popular option for travelers who want to skip the youth hostel. Hands-on hosts often become built-in tour guides, or at the very least, useful insider resources. There's no charge to crash at someone else's house, but the catch is that you're expected to reciprocate with another participant; while CouchSurfing encourages but doesn't require it, GlobalFreeloaders does. Worried about security? Word-of-mouth vouching systems, personal profiles, and an optional verification system requiring a credit card are some of the methods in place to keep things kosher.

A newer service takes things one step further, letting hosts rent out air beds. **AirBed & Breakfast**'s peer-to-peer service lets people rent out any available space from an inflatable mattress to a spare bedroom—usually for $50.00 to $100.00 a night. It currently covers more than 644 cities in 69 countries, and it became an especially popular option for Washington, DC-area locals to earn some extra cash when travelers flooded the city for President Barack Obama's inauguration. Unlike other peer-to-peer services like Craigslist.org or local newspapers, this site allows online reservations and payment through PayPal.

A similar service called **Roomorama** offers apartment rentals in cities like New York City, Boston, Chicago, and Toronto. Renters are vetted via a rating system and payments are handled online.

Then there is the ultimate in free stays: home exchanges. This is a one-to-one swap between you and a home owner in another part of the country or world. Sites like **Homeexchange.com, IntervacUS.com,** and **HomeLink.org** help you arrange to switch homes for a few days, weeks, or even longer—depending on your agreement. The stay may be free, but online membership can cost as much as $100.00 a year to post and respond to listings.

An old-school service in the travel world is **Servas International,** which has been promoting "understanding, tolerance and world peace" since 1949. Guests can stay short-term in member homes located in about 130 countries.

▶▶ CouchSurfing.com, www.couchsurfing.com

▶▶ GlobalFreeloaders.com, www.globalfreeloaders.com

▶▶ AirBed & Breakfast, www.airbedandbreakfast.com

▶▶ Roomorama, www.roomorama.com

▶▶ Home Exchange, www.homeexchange.com

▶▶ Intervac, www.intervacus.com

▶▶ HomeLink International, www.homelink.org

▶▶ Servas International, www.servas.org

> Tip: Hostels are no longer limited to 20-something backpackers. They can range from the dreaded 10-person dorm room to private rooms with en suite bathrooms and, as a bonus, some can be found in truly unusual locations. Think of it as an added adventure. For example, the Point Montara Lighthouse in Northern California is a working lighthouse that sleeps 45 in rooms starting at $22.00 a night; in England, you can sleep in a water-powered corn mill at the Winchester Mill Hostel; and at the Jumbo Hostel at Stockholm, you can sleep in a real Boeing 747-200, starting at $45.00 a night (the luxury suite in the cockpit will cost you more). Check Hostelling International to find traditional and unusual hostels worldwide.

▶▶ Hostelling International, www.hihostels.com

Vacation-Home/Villa Rentals

If you're paying $200.00 and up per night for a hotel room, you might want to consider vacation-home or villa rentals, which have the potential to cut your trip costs enormously. Not only do you save on extras like dining out, tipping, and parking, but you also get to experience some local flavor. And the savings potential increases dramatically when you're traveling in a group—so if you've always dreamed of vacationing with friends in a vineyard or of having a family reunion in Tuscany, this is how to do it and save.

> Tip: Villa rates in Italy and France drop in September, and the weather is still great.

Take a look at these sample rates from some of the top vacation-rental resources for a mid-August (early harvest season) stay in Napa, California. For comparison, a one-bedroom suite with a kitchen at Embassy Suites near downtown Napa starts at $259.00 a night per room (sleeps two people).

HomeAway, an Austin, Texas-based company that owns sites like HomeAway.com, VRBO.com, VacationRentals.com, and GreatRentals.com, has virtually cornered the online vacation-rental market. A free guarantee gets you up to a $5,000.00 reimbursement and alternative accommodations if a listing turns out to be illegitimate. A two-bedroom house called Adler's Nest near downtown Napa is listed at $250.00 a night, or $125.00 per couple.

Zonder is a relatively new site with the added bonus of a 24/7 support line—if there is a price discrepancy, they'll refund the difference, and if your rental property was misrepresented, they'll find alternate accommodations or issue a refund. A three-bedroom, two-bathroom home with a pool near downtown Napa starts at $354.00 a night, which breaks down to $118.00 per couple per night.

Beautiful Places is a service that works only with luxury properties, most of which feature several bedrooms, gourmet kitchens, and pools. A four-bedroom, five-and-a-half-bathroom two-story starts at $5,950.00 per week, which breaks down to $212.50 per night for four couples.

▶▶ Home Away, www.homeaway.com

▶▶ Vacation Rentals by Owner, www.vrbo.com

▶▶ Vacation Rentals, www.vacationrentals.com

▶▶ Great Rentals, www.greatrentals.com

▶▶ Zonder, www.zonder.com

▶▶ Beautiful Places, www.beautiful-places.com

▽ Additional Resources

Parker Villas, www.parkervillas.com
Rentals.com, http://vacation.rentals.com
BookIt (specializes in consolidating travel deals), www.bookit.com

CHAPTER 4

RENTING A CAR

MANY PEOPLE MAKE THE MISTAKE of thinking that the advertised, quoted rate is what they will pay when they rent a car. In a robust economy, they'll be disappointed to learn how much more they will end up paying. During an economic meltdown, if they know how to play the car-rental game, they'll be pleasantly surprised to learn they'll pay less than the official rates. And, with a little advance planning, it could be substantially less.

> **Tip:** When it comes to online booking, I often have good luck with "opaque" features on sites like Priceline.com and Hotwire.com, where you don't know which company you're booking with until the final stage. These companies partner only with major car-rental companies, though, so you can rest assured that you're booking with a reputable agency.

I've generally found that of all the transactions involved with the travel industry, renting a car offers the most flexibility in negotiating a deal. A car sitting unused in a lot means that no revenue is being generated, so car-rental agencies are more likely to release that car at a discounted price. As is the case when negotiating hotel rates, the key is to call the local agency, not the toll-free reservation number.

The best day and time to call for a rental is Saturday morning. Car-rental companies consistently overbook their fleets, and by Saturday, they'll know how many cars haven't been picked up. Because most advance car rentals don't require the booker to give a credit card number, failing to show up doesn't cost them anything.

Before you start your negotiations, check online for some general prices. Then, once you have someone on the phone, find out the basics: How much you will pay in taxes and fees; whether or not there is unlimited mileage, including out-of-state miles (if not, try to get that worked into your total fee); whether you will be charged for an "upgrade" if the type of car you request isn't available. And lastly, ask for the weekly rate, which tends to be cheaper than the daily rate; if you're renting for more than 4 days, try to negotiate for a weekly rate.

> Tip: One surefire way to save money on your next road trip is to maximize your gas mileage. When you drive more than 60 mph, your fuel economy decreases significantly. If you're driving on a highway, use the cruise control: a constant speed (at 60 mph or less) will use fuel far more economically than accelerating and braking frequently. And reduce your load as much as possible—more weight requires more gas.

Car-Rental Insurance

Should you pay for a collision damage waiver (CDW) or not? This optional car-rental insurance can tack an additional 20 to 25 percent onto your total price. My advice here is to check your credit card policy. For example, if you pay for your car rental with an American Express card, a CDW is included; however, other credit card policies vary, so it's crucial to read the fine print. But even if your credit card provider claims it's included, you may only be getting secondary—not primary— insurance, which kicks in only if the demand exceeds the limit of your primary auto insurance. So if your rental car gets dinged or scratched, the damage will fall within your primary insurance's deductible, and then guess who's paying out of pocket?

In addition, personal auto insurance and credit card coverage generally don't apply to travel outside of the United States (sometimes not even in Canada or Mexico). Some foreign car-rental agen-

> **Tip:** With most car-rental companies, returning the car even an hour late can incur a charge by the hour for an extra day. If you think you're running late, call the agency ahead of time to plead your case. If you get charged, discuss it with a manager right then and there. The longer you wait, the harder it will be to fix—don't wait until you get home to demand a refund.

cies have specific insurance policies unique to their countries—such as "windshield coverage" in New Zealand (where gravel roads tend to ding windshields). So yes, if you're driving outside of the United States, you can save money by skipping the extra insurance, but it's not something I would recommend otherwise.

However, I do think you can skip something called personal effects coverage (PEC). It sounds great in theory, because it costs only a couple of dollars a day and covers personal items stolen from your rental car. But that's only if the car is locked and there is evidence of forcible entry, in which case you'll have to file a police report. Of course, there is usually a cap on how much you can claim and, like airlines, rental agencies have a list of items that are excluded from coverage—everything from cash to airline tickets. The good news, and another reason to skip this option, is that in many cases, these things are already covered by your home owner's or renter's insurance policy.

> **Tip:** Don't present your debit card when picking up your rental car. Most companies will put an authorization hold of up to $500.00 on the card, which can take up to 2 weeks to be deposited back into your account, potentially leaving you wiped out during your travels.

Lastly, there is something called supplemental liability insurance (SLI), which costs about $10.00 a day and covers up to $1 million. But that only comes into play if you cause a massive pileup with damages reaching several hundred thousand dollars. My advice? Skip it.

Auto-Repositioning Deals

I look at most rental-car fleets like flocks of migrating birds. At different times and during different seasons, those birds have to head south, north, east, or west, depending on demand. There is one scenario in which car-rental companies will practically pay you to drive their cars. It's called auto repositioning, and it involves cars that need to be relocated to elsewhere in the country.

With repositioning, there is no rental fee and you even get the first tank of gas for free. All you have to put down is a refundable deposit (usually about $350.00) and pay for the remainder of your fuel, lodging, and food. The biggest drawback, of course, is that it's a one-way trip, so you're responsible for getting yourself back home. (But with so many airlines now selling discounted one-way tickets, you'll still be way ahead of the game.)

The time you want to look for drive-away deals is in the spring, when companies move their fleets from destinations like Florida to the Northeast, and vice versa in the fall. Although most companies do offer these deals, they're not widely publicized or frequent, so your best bet is to call local offices to ask about repositioning deals. However, one great resource is **Auto**

Driveaway, one of the biggest vehicle delivery providers that moves fleets of cars and offers door-to-door vehicle delivery. Or simply check the Yellow Pages for local car-moving services—they may be looking for drivers.

If you're looking for a family getaway, how about an RV drive-away? **Cruise America** offers one-way deals for as little as $24.00 per day, and **El Monte RV** takes at least 70 percent off its regular RV rates for some one-way trips for the first 14 days.

▶▶ Auto Driveaway, www.autodriveaway.com

▶▶ Cruise America, www.cruiseamerica.com

▶▶ El Monte RV, www.elmonterv.com

Overseas Delivery

Here's a way to get a free vacation—just buy a car overseas! If you purchase a car directly from the factory in Europe, the company will actually pay for part of your trip. Audi, BMW, Mercedes, Porsche, Saab, and Volvo have been doing this for years. (Mercedes pioneered the concept more than 40 years ago.)

How does it work? You purchase your car at a local dealer, but take delivery at the factory. With Mercedes, you get optional two-for-one airfare, a free night at a hotel, a 7 percent discount on the total price of the car, a tour of the company's factory in Sindelfingen, Germany, and 15 days of European road insurance so you can hit the open road with your new car. Mercedes then ships the car for free to your local dealership. (Caution: It can take several months.)

Volvo's deal is an appealing one, offering two free round-trip tickets to the factory in Gothenburg, Sweden, a 1-night stay at the Radisson SAS Scandinavia Hotel, and 4 to 8 percent off the total price of the car. Volvo will register your new vehicle and walk you through the process of obtaining 2 weeks of European auto insurance for your driving vacation, and, perhaps best of all, you get a traditional Swedish lunch of meatballs and lingonberry sauce.

> **Tip:** Don't fall victim to this common travel scheme: Online scammers advertise something called an international driver's license and claim that you need one to drive overseas or that having one means you can avoid parking tickets and fines. No such thing exists. There is, however, something called an International Driving Permit (IDP). An IDP is not a license. It's a form of identification that translates the information on an American driver's license into 10 languages and is accepted in more than 150 countries. IDPs are required if you're driving more than 300 miles into Mexico or more than 50 miles into Canada. Only two organizations are authorized to sell IDPs: AAA and the National Auto Club.

Return your car to Gothenburg and Volvo will ship it to the United States for free within a few months.

Intrigued? Each company outlines its overseas delivery program on its Web site, or you can find out details through your local dealer.

▽ Additional Resources

United States Department of Energy, www.fueleconomy.gov
Gas Buddy, www.gasbuddy.com
AAA Fuel Cost Calculator, www.fuelcostcalculator.com

> **Tip:** Don't get hit by an unexpected fine. Several European cities now have "restricted driving zones" that are great sources of revenue in the form of traffic violations. In London, there's a fee to drive in the downtown Congestion Charging zone weekdays between 7:00 a.m. and 6:00 p.m. Check out www.cclondon.com to find out where those zones are and pay the fee ahead of time. In Italy, restricted zones are in most cities' historic centers. They're usually marked by poor signage, and the rules can vary: You can drive but not park; you can't enter after 8:00 p.m.; you can't enter even on a pogo stick on the night of a full moon. It can take up to a year for a ticket to reach you or your car-rental agency, and unfortunately you can't claim ignorance to get out of the fine. So plan ahead and contact your hotel—if it's located within a restricted driving zone, it may be able to issue you a temporary permit.

CHAPTER 5

CRUISING ON A DIME

THE RECENT ECONOMIC meltdown has created an unexpected silver lining in at least one segment of the travel industry: cruising.

And for those with a sense of history, that wasn't a big surprise. After the tragic events of September 11, 2001, the cruise industry was perhaps the only segment of the overall travel business that was able to adapt quickly to the almost instant downturn in overseas travel by Americans. Why? Because the cruise industry could literally reposition its assets. And that's exactly what happened— cruise ships were moved from Europe, Asia, and South America to about 17 US ports. Cities that didn't even know they had ports were suddenly entering the cruise business.

As a result, reaching your cruise ship no longer required an overseas flight, with ships instead departing from accessible "drive-to" destinations across the United States.

That was the good news for the cruise industry.

Still, they had to fill cabins. Though there was widespread discounting, the hope was that the new drive-to cruise market would result in cruise lines starting to enjoy healthy profits. It was slow at first, but in the 7 years after 9/11, many cruise lines have embarked on ambitious shipbuilding programs, constructing megaliners with room for 2,400 or more passengers and 1,100-plus crew members. As cruising became more popular, they filled cabins while keeping prices robust.

And then, as the economy turned sour in late 2008, the cruise lines once again faced the challenge of filling cabins. And the discounts followed.

Other than that immediate price benefit, there are other compelling reasons that cruising is affordable during these tough times. When you book a cruise, you're hedging your dollar. For instance, once you lock into that European cruise, it doesn't matter if the dollar later tanks against the euro, because the majority of your meals and entertainment is already paid for.

But there are some drawbacks: Once you dock at your European port, you're going to be buying everything in euros. Also, cruise ships aren't exactly all-inclusive—you still have to pay for drinks, meals at onboard specialty restaurants, some activities, and other sundries that can really add up.

When to Go

Like other types of travel, cruising has certain periods when fewer people are traveling and you can get even more insane discounts. The best times are the 3 weeks between Thanksgiving and Christmas, the first half of January, April, most of May (excluding Memorial Day), and the first 2 weeks of June, when most schools are still in session.

On LastMinuteCruises.com, a search performed in early November 2008 for a 3-day cruise to the Bahamas showed the drop-dead lowest rate ($129.00 per person) was for a departure only 2 weeks away. But, looking ahead, it increased by a whopping 170 percent for a departure in early June 2009 and by 209 percent for a July departure.

Of course, different regions have different high periods. If you're headed to the Caribbean, hurricane season (June 1

> Tip: If a cruise-booking site's search feature allows it, choose your destination but leave the preferred departure date open. That way, you'll be able to see what time periods are cheaper than others.

through November 30, peaking from August through October) will have some great deals—just make sure you get travel insurance, and don't be disappointed if your ship gets rerouted and doesn't hit every scheduled port.

For European cruises, look for companies that have year-round departures, like Norwegian Cruise Line, so you can take advantage of January deals (just make sure you bring a jacket). A trip on the *Norwegian Jade* from Barcelona to Morocco and Portugal is about $400.00 cheaper in January than in March.

▶▶ LastMinuteCruises.com, www.lastminutecruises.com

Cruise Consolidators

Cruise consolidators work just like ticket brokers—they buy big blocks of cabins at a bulk rate, then resell them to customers at a discount.

As Pat Webb of California–based GalaxSea Cruise and Tours told me, "In good times, cruise lines don't need us. In bad times, we're a valuable asset." Look at it this way: Say a cruise line needs to dump 20 cabins. If they put those rooms on a major Web site like Expedia.com at rock-bottom prices, they'll be inundated with calls from unhappy already-booked passengers demanding the same rate.

So instead, they let a cruise consolidator release those rooms—quietly. The consolidator distributes the information to private lists of regular clients, select e-mail lists, and sometimes online. Through a reputable consolidator, you can find deals that cost as little as $50.00 a day.

Another benefit of using one of these companies is that they specialize in cruises. So, along with the potential savings, you're likely to be matched up with a cruise line and an itinerary that fit your needs rather than searching blindly on the Internet.

▶▶ Cruise Brothers, 800-827-7779, www.cruisebrothers.com

▶▶ GalaxSea Cruise and Tours, 800-662-5450, www.cruisestar.com

▶▶ LowestCruisePrices.com, 888-615-7447,
www.lowestcruiseprices.com

▶▶ World Wide Cruises, 800-882-9000, www.wwcruises.com

Last-Minute Cruises

The term "last minute" can be somewhat misleading. Back in the 1970s, you could literally go to a dock and hop aboard a departing cruise ship for half-price, but those days are long, long gone. Now, cruise lines have to close the passenger manifest (the list of passengers and crew onboard) 24 to 96 hours before sailing, so the most last-minute you might get is about 1 week in advance—but it's often more like 30 to 60 days.

In most cases, travel agents aren't going to be able to help much with late bookings. They have to deal with red tape and payment logistics that make booking last-minute cruises not worth the hassle. But the Internet is a whole other story.

Like cruise consolidators, last-minute cruising sites are essentially dumping grounds for the cruise-lines. Web sites like LastMinuteCruises.com have developed solid reputations among consumers and are trusted sources for cruise line executives who send out waves of discounted sailings.

If you want to know about the best deals, familiarize yourself with a last-minute site and then sign up for its newsletter or e-mail blast. Sometimes, when the supply of discounted cabins is very limited, it isn't feasible to post those rates online for all to see. Being on a mailing list ensures that you actually.get to see those deeply gouged rates.

Saving Money on Shore Excursions

One of the biggest—if not *the* biggest—profit generators for cruise lines is shore excursions. But you can save money if you plan them right.

Shore excursions are a big part of cruising in terms of experience and price. After all, cruise lines don't make money filling rooms; their revenue comes from the extras that you pay for: beverages, photographs, and money lost in gambling. But you can save by booking your shore excursion with an independent operator—*not* through the cruise line.

Take as an example the ever-popular jungle canopy tour in Puerto Vallarta, Mexico: You can book it through a cruise line such as Norwegian for $115.00 per person. Or, you can book directly with the provider, Los Veranos Canopy Tour, for $79.00, plus about $4.00 for a taxi ride to the central office.

In Ocho Rios, Jamaica, a Jeep safari tour of Dunns River Falls will cost you about $99.00 if you book through a cruise line such as Princess. Compare that with about $70.00 when you book through Viator, a San Francisco-based booking company that works with local operators.

And, if you do a little investigating, you'll find out that both Princess and Viator book the Dunns River Falls tour with local operator Chukka Caribbean Adventures, which charges $73.00. While the folks from Chukka refused to give us a definitive answer on whether cruisers can "officially" book shore excursions through them, there's nothing to stop you from trying. As long as you can get yourself to and from the pick-up point, you're in the clear.

So the lesson here is: Do it on your own! You'll save even more, whether you're interested in activities like shopping and dining, taking a city bus tour, or engaging in ultra-touristy excursions like a gondola ride. Trust me, the locals in port cities cater to travelers, so you'll be fighting off vendors as soon as you get off the ship.

A word of warning, though: If you're late returning from a shore excursion that wasn't booked through the cruise line, they have no obligation to hold the ship for you!

▶▶ Los Veranos Canopy Tour, www.canopytours-vallarta.com

▶▶ Viator, www.viator.com

Safely Be Your Own Travel Agent

The big trick is finding a tour company that's not some fly-by-night operation. You don't want to book online and then be stood up at the port or have a mediocre experience that's not worth the money you paid. Here are some other things to consider before you sign up with an outside vendor.

- Online, look for a tour operator that's accredited by the Cruise Lines International Association or the American Society of Travel Agents.
- Cruise lines usually subcontract their shore activities to third-party providers (a Holland America employee, for example, isn't guiding your excursion). They evaluate local operators and verify that they have the proper licensing, equipment, and insurance, as well as good safety records. So if you don't book through your cruise line, it's up to you to request that kind of information.
- If you arrange your excursion through a booking agency (instead of directly with the operator), find out their vetting process. Viator, for example, has field agents who make sure each subcontractor has the proper licenses and insurance.
- Ask for some sort of guarantee when you book. For example, the company Mexico Fun, which operates tours throughout Mexico via sites like Puertovallartatours.com and Playadelcarmentours.com, offers a "no port, no pay" guarantee. If your cruise doesn't stop at that port for any reason, you get a full refund.

- Because you can't check out foreign companies with organizations like the Better Business Bureau, user-review sites like TripAdvisor.com and message boards on cruise sites like Cruisecritic.com are an invaluable resource for finding out about the real experiences of real people.

▶▶ Puerto Vallarta Tours, www.puertovallartatours.com

▶▶ Playa del Carmen Tours, www.playadelcarmentours.com

▶▶ Cruise Critic, www.cruisecritic.com

Drive-To Ports

The fact that the cruise industry is paying so much attention to drive-to ports is really going to pay off in this sluggish economy. With ships moving to ports that are a little closer to home, you'll get to skip out on paying for an expensive plane ticket.

Now, we're not just talking about Miami, New York City, and Los Angeles. How about Baltimore, San Francisco, New Orleans? And how about major cruise lines like Royal Caribbean and Norwegian? That's right—big companies are moving their ships from Europe and South America and placing them squarely in the United States to create more localized itineraries.

Check out some of these surprise drive-to options, based on schedules for 2009.

PORT	CRUISE LINES AND DESTINATIONS
Baltimore, Maryland (www.cruisemaryland.com)	**Norwegian Cruise Line:** Bermuda; Norfolk, Virginia **Royal Caribbean Cruise Lines:** Canada/New England, Bermuda, the Caribbean **Carnival Cruise Lines:** Bahamas
Boston, Massachusetts (www.massport.com/ports/cruis.html)	**Norwegian:** Bermuda **Holland America Line:** Canada
Cape Liberty, New Jersey (www.cruiseliberty.com)	**Royal Caribbean:** Bermuda, the Caribbean
Charleston, South Carolina (www.port-of-charleston.com)	**Norwegian:** Bermuda, the Caribbean

PORT	CRUISE LINES AND DESTINATIONS
Galveston, Texas (www.portofgalveston.com)	**Carnival:** Mexico, the Caribbean **Royal Caribbean:** Mexico, the Caribbean
Jacksonville, Florida (www.jaxport.com)	**Carnival:** Bahamas
Mobile, Alabama (www.shipmobile.com)	**Carnival:** the Caribbean
New Orleans, Louisiana (www.portno.com)	**Carnival:** the Caribbean **Norwegian:** the Caribbean
Norfolk, Virginia (www.cruisenorfolk.org)	**Princess Cruises:** Bahamas **Royal Caribbean:** the Caribbean, Bermuda
Philadelphia, Pennsylvania (www.cruisephilly.com)	**Norwegian:** the Caribbean, New England/Canada
San Diego, California (www.sandiegocruiseport.com)	**Holland America:** Panama Canal, Mexico, Mexican Riviera, Sea of Cortez, Hawaii **Carnival:** Mexico, Mexican Riviera **Royal Caribbean:** Panama Canal, Valparaiso, Mexican Riviera, Alaska **Celebrity Cruises:** Pacific Northwest, Panama Canal, Hawaii
San Francisco, California (www.sfport.com)	**Princess:** Mexico, Alaska **Silversea Cruises:** Alaska **Norwegian:** Mexico
Seattle, Washington (www.portseattle.org)	**Princess:** Alaska **Celebrity:** Alaska, Pacific Northwest **Royal Caribbean:** Alaska **Norwegian:** Alaska **Holland America:** Alaska
Tampa, Florida (www.tampaport.com)	**Carnival:** the Caribbean, Mexico **Holland America:** the Caribbean, Mexico **Royal Caribbean:** Mexico, Central America

Taking the Slow Boat

Historically, taking longer cruises by freighter has never been the best bargain out there, but if you have the time, that option has also become economically viable.

Most cargo ships can accommodate up to 12 passengers, but chances are you'll be one of only two or three leisure passengers onboard a working ship. The average price is about $100.00 per day (though prices are usually quoted in euros) to join the trip.

That's less expensive than a traditional cruise ship, but less economical—in terms of both time and money—than air travel.

Traveling by freight ship means you're purposely choosing to take the "slow boat," hitching a ride alongside cargo that's being transported from point A to point B, to C, to D, and sometimes back the other way.

Depending on the route, you can sail for anywhere from 14 days to 14 weeks—although if you want to shorten a long trip, you can simply arrange to get off at a port and fly home.

Common routes include:

- Transatlantic from New York or Halifax, Nova Scotia, to the Mediterranean; and from Europe to Central or South America.
- Transpacific from Los Angeles to Australia or New Zealand; and from Los Angeles or Seattle to the Far East.
- Down the East Coast from New York to South America.

If you've really got some time, how about a 52-day trip from Europe to East Asia? You'd start in France, sail south in the Atlantic and into the Mediterranean, snake along the coast of Africa and through the Suez Canal into the Red Sea, and across the Indian Ocean into Southeast Asia and then up to East Asia—with 15 port stops in all.

The rule of thumb is flexibility. You may spend only a few hours at each port—though usually you're there for 8 to 24 hours—and there's no guarantee you'll be there during daylight. However, longer-haul trips, particularly ones traveling around the world, tend to stop at ports for a few days at a time. Keep in mind that ports of call can change according to weather conditions, port congestion, and other factors.

Also know that your day-to-day experience won't be like that on a traditional cruise ship. First of all, cargo ships, usually between

485 and 965 feet long, tend to be smaller than cruise ships. Royal Caribbean's *Voyager of the Seas,* by comparison, is about 1,020 feet long. While modern freighters are typically clean and comfortable and have large cabins and private bathrooms, you may find yourself climbing over winches and cranes while on deck.

In terms of amenities, there are no formal dinners, no drinks on the Lido deck, and no slot machines. Some ships do have small gyms and sometimes even a sauna or a pool (although one traveler reported that the pool would occasionally be drained to hold overflowing banana shipments). So be sure to bring your own entertainment, and look forward to spending long days lounging and taking in the sea air on a (small) deck.

Most cargo ships won't take on passengers who are older than 79 to 82 years and require all passengers to submit a statement of good health signed by a physician.

Sample trips:

Ship: *Hansa Flensburg*
Route: Transpacific
Details: 54 days, £80.00 (about $100.00) per person per day
Ports of call: Los Angeles (Day 1); Tauranga, New Zealand (Day 15); Sydney (Day 19), Melbourne (Day 22), and Adelaide, Australia (Day 24); Auckland, New Zealand (Day 30); Papeete, Tahiti (Day 36); Ensenada, Mexico (Day 42); San Francisco (Day 46); Seattle (Day 49); Vancouver (Day 51); Los Angeles (Day 54)

Ship: CSAV *Hamburgo*
Route: South America
Details: 42 days, around £70.00 (about $88.00) per person per day
Ports of call: Elizabeth, New Jersey (Day 1); Baltimore (Day 2); Charleston, South Carolina (Day 4); Port

Everglades, Florida (Day 5); Cartagena, Colombia (Day 9); Panama Canal (Day 10); Guayaquil, Ecuador (Day 14); Callao, Peru (Day 16); San Antonio (Day 20) and San Vicente, Chile (Day 23); Callao, Peru (Day 27); Guayaquil, Ecuador (Day 31); Panama Canal (Day 32); Cartagena, Colombia (Day 35); Port Everglades, Florida (Day 40); Elizabeth, New Jersey (Day 42)

▶▶ Freighter World Cruises, 800-531-7774, www.freighterworld.com

▶▶ Maris Freighter & Specialty Cruises, 800-996-2747, www.freightercruises.com

Repositioning Cruises

Now, these are a real bargain if you have time and flexibility. Repositioning cruises usually take place in the fall and spring, when cruise companies are moving ships to different ports for the new season. So, a ship that sails Alaska in the summer months may move to the South Pacific for the winter. Instead of sailing with empty ships, cruise lines invite passengers to join the one-way journey, and often for deeply discounted rates. And the good news is that you'll still get the same dining options, entertainment, spa services, and other onboard amenities as on normal cruises.

However, there are different types of repositioning cruises. You're likely to save the most on a transatlantic repositioning, say from Boston to Southampton, England. These trips involve more days at sea and fewer days at port, meaning fewer port fees to pay, and they tend to run a little longer than traditional cruises (usually more than 2 weeks).

The biggest drawback of a repositioning cruise is that it's a one-way trip, so booking your return flight is up to you. To save on that cost, look for ships that are repositioning from one North

American port to another—one of which should ideally be a drive-to port. Otherwise, you'll be stuck booking yet another one-way plane ticket.

Repositioning Close to Home

Every year around Halloween, Royal Caribbean's *Jewel of the Seas* moves from Boston to Miami, with stops in San Juan, Puerto Rico; Charlotte Amalie, St. Thomas; St. Croix, US Virgin Islands; and Oranjestad, Aruba, along the way. The price for this 10-night cruise starts at a cool $899.00 per person (not including fuel charges and other fees).

In the spring, Holland America's MS *Maasdam* repositions from Fort Lauderdale, Florida, to Montreal. This 15-day trip starts at $1,209.00 on CruiseBrothers.com (that's $80.06 a day) and stops in Charleston, South Carolina; Newport, Rhode Island; Bar Harbor, Maine; Halifax and Sydney, Nova Scotia; Charlottetown, Prince Edward Island; and Gaspé, Sept-Îles, Saguenay, and Quebec City, Quebec. Not a bad way to see the Eastern seaboard!

▶▶ Cruise Brothers, www.cruisebrothers.com

> Tip: Some cruise lines, like Royal Caribbean, have a special "repositioning" section on their Web sites where you can find these deals. Others don't separate them, so look for one-way routes that have only one or two departure dates a year—and you've found yourself a repositioning cruise!

More Bang for Your Travel Buck?

In some cases, particularly when the trip involves several port stops, the price of a repositioning cruise may be comparable with that of a traditional one. But what you're getting is more bang for your travel buck—an eclectic mix of exotic ports that you might never hit otherwise.

(continued on page 52)

Solo Travel

One is the loneliest number, especially in the travel industry. Historically, when it comes to price discrimination, solo travelers have felt it the most—they know the pain of the dreaded single-supplement fee.

Cruise lines don't make money from empty beds, so they charge single travelers more to make up the difference—in some cases, it's 50 to 100 percent of the per-person double-occupancy fee. Why? It's all about the cruise lines generating onboard revenue, and each person is projected (translation: expected) to drink, eat, go on shore excursions, play at the casino, relax at the spa—all things that are otherwise known as *ka-ching!*

But now on cruises, rates are dropping so much that even the single supplement is suddenly affordable. Example: On one recent 7-day Western Caribbean cruise, cabins were going for $249.00, which works out to $35.00 a night, including meals. Double that price if you're traveling solo and it jumps to $70.00 a night for the cruise and meals; could you even stay at home for that price?

Prices are so low, in fact, that I know of a number of cases where folks strapped for cash leased out their apartments for a month and booked four consecutive cruises on the same exact itinerary and actually saved money—and ate very well!

But there are other ways to benefit from a drop in prices and still not pay the single supplement.

Your first step is to find a roommate. Holland America will match you with another solo cruiser of the same gender—provided that there is one on your trip. Yes, you're going to be sharing very close quarters with a stranger, but you need to put things in perspective. How much time will you be spending in your cabin in any 24-hour period? Not much, other than to shower and sleep. And that's the point. You find a roommate, save even more money, and adjust.

Other cruise lines, such as Princess, Crystal, and Costa, work with a company called Singles At Sea for singles-themed trips. They, too, have a match program to help you save on costs. Single-occupancy cabins are available on some ships, but you're still going to be charged a "single fee," which will be significantly higher than what you'd pay if you were sharing a room and paying half the double-occupancy rate.

If you're into the meeting game, several other companies arrange singles cruises aboard regularly scheduled cruises: the Boca Raton, Florida-based Singles Travel International will either find you a roommate or cover the supplement fee themselves. All Singles Travel organizes singles cruises and tours and offers an optional roommate-matching service. Other reputable solo travel companies include the members-only O Solo Mio and Adventures for Singles.

Prefer to find your own roommate? Cruisemates.com has a message board so cruisers can match up itineraries. Other travel-focused social networking sites like Where Are You Now? and Travelocity's Meet Me In . . . are good resources for single travelers trying to coordinate with friends or family.

When it comes to hotels, the single-supplement fee is a little more nebulous. Hotels are becoming more transparent with their rates, but never assume: Always ask if a quoted hotel price is per person or per room. And if a hotel has single rooms available, they'll be cheaper than staying in a double room by yourself, but more expensive than the per-person rate for the double room.

Single-supplement fees are also big with tour groups. Companies like Vantage Deluxe World Travel, Intrepid Travel, and Tauck Tours tend to be solo-friendly, either matching you up with a roommate or reducing the supplement fee on certain trips.

▶▶ Singles at Sea, www.singlesatsea.com

▶▶ Singles Travel International, www.singlestravelintl.com

▶▶ All Singles Travel, www.allsinglestravel.com

▶▶ O Solo Mio, www.osolomio.com

▶▶ Adventures for Singles, www.adventuresforsingles.com

▶▶ Where Are You Now? www.wayn.com

▶▶ Travelocity's Meet Me In . . . , www.travelocity.com/meetmein

▶▶ Vantage Deluxe World Travel, www.vantagetravel.com

▶▶ Intrepid Travel, www.intrepidtravel.com

▶▶ Tauck Tours, www.tauck.com

Each spring, Princess Cruises' *Diamond Princess* departs for a 22-night transpacific cruise from Beijing to Vancouver with a whopping 12 ports of call: Beijing and Dalian, China; Kagoshima, Japan; Pusan, South Korea; Vladivostok, Russia; Muroran, Japan; and Anchorage, College Fjord, Glacier Bay National Park, Skagway, Juneau, and Ketchikan, Alaska, before landing in Vancouver. The price? $1,869.00 per person, or $595.00 a week.

No comparable regular cruise hits all of those ports, but a 1-week cruise that travels only to Alaska from Seattle or San Francisco starts at $599.00—about same per-week price for a quarter of the destinations.

A little closer to home, Royal Caribbean's *Enchantment of the Seas* sails in November from Fort Lauderdale, Florida, to Colón, Panama, via Ocho Rios, Jamaica; Santa Marta and Cartagena, Colombia; Puerto Limón, Costa Rica; and finally, Colón. Not a bad group of destinations! And the starting price for this 8-day journey is $399.00 per person, plus up to $140.00 as a fuel charge.

By comparison, a regular 7-day Royal Caribbean cruise to the Caribbean would cost you about the same price, but you stop only in ultra-touristy spots like Miami; Labadee, Haiti; Ocho Rios, Jamaica; George Town, Grand Cayman; and Cozumel, Mexico.

Call me crazy, but I'd much rather spend the same amount of money to travel to Jamaica, Central America, and South America than to cruise from one Caribbean island to another.

▽ Additional Resources:

Cruise Direct, www.cruisedirect.com
Cruise 411, www.cruise411.com
Last Minute Travel, www.lastminutetravel.com
Priceline, www.priceline.com

CHAPTER 6

FAMILY TRAVEL

EVEN IN GREAT, healthy economies, family travel is the great budget buster. And now more than ever, a family's ability to travel is not only being challenged by high costs, but also by limited resources. Does that mean you need to stay at home this year? Not even close.

For one thing, family loyalty is perhaps the biggest explanation for why Thanksgiving is the biggest travel holiday of the year, and why we brave overcrowded airports during a snowstorm to arrive just in time for Christmas Eve. A recent survey from Kayak.com showed that even in these tough economic times, 39 percent of travelers refused to sacrifice their plans in order to save money.

But you have to factor in the hassle and expense of schlepping kids along for the ride. I feel real sympathy for parents who have to pack up half their house and then pay to check four suitcases and a car seat at $15.00 to $50.00 per piece.

> **Tip:** I always recommend purchasing an airplane seat for children under the age of 2, even though the FAA doesn't require it. Yeah, it's expensive, but it's not safe to keep an infant or toddler on your lap while you're flying.

Then there's the fact that families generally travel during peak seasons—i.e., when the kids are out of school. Factor in the expenses of meals, activities, and transportation once you're at your destination—it adds up. Fast.

It's for those reasons that families have optimized the art of traveling on a budget: Skip the expensive flights and drive to someplace close to home; forget about fine dining and make your own meals; and forgo pricey hotels in favor of EconoLodges or, better yet, campsites.

First and foremost, you'll want to take advantage of the most basic of hotel freebies: breakfast.

From **Hampton Inn,** which is thought to have been the first US hotel chain to offer free breakfast, to **Holiday Inn,** which claims to have pioneered the kids-eat-free concept, to continental buffets at **La Quinta,** free food abounds at budget properties.

So why wouldn't you expect it as part of your room rate? Even if it's not automatically included in the price, try negotiating with a manager—you may be surprised by how easily you can finagle a free breakfast or credit to use toward meals.

Look for kids-eat-free promotions at hotels like **Hyatt** and **Marriott**—they're not permanent deals, but as hotels vie for your travel dollars, expect to see this more and more. At participating properties, **Hilton's** program called My Little Hilton features a free children's menu for kids up to age 10 and half-priced second rooms for kids (otherwise children stay free in the room with parents).

Another great option is to skip the traditional hotel room altogether and opt for an extended-stay suite. Not only do you get more space, but you can also save by making your own meals and snacks in the suite's kitchenette. Just don't overlook one important factor—there has to be a grocery or convenience store nearby.

Marriott's extended-stay brands, **Residence Inn** and **TownePlace Suites,** start at around $100.00 a night for studio, one-

> Tip: Think local when it comes to family-friendly activities. That can mean looking for neighborhood playgrounds, storytelling sessions at the library, or events at the local YMCA.

bedroom, and two-bedroom suites with full kitchens. Residence Inn takes it a step further by offering free breakfast and a grocery delivery service. **Embassy Suites** includes full kitchens in its suites and a free breakfast that actually includes made-to-order omelets. **Staybridge Suites** offers both a breakfast buffet and a continental breakfast packed up for you as early as 5:30 a.m. to take "on the go," which can work out well for families trying to pack in a full day of activities.

▶▶ Hampton Inn, http://hamptoninn1.hilton.com

▶▶ Holiday Inn, www.holidayinn.com

▶▶ La Quinta, www.lq.com

▶▶ Hyatt, www.hyatt.com

▶▶ Marriott, www.marriott.com

▶▶ Hilton, www.hilton.com

▶▶ Residence Inn, www.residenceinn.com

▶▶ TownePlace Suites, www.towneplacesuites.com

▶▶ Embassy Suites, http://embassysuites1.hilton.com

▶▶ Staybridge Suites, www.staybridgesuites.com

Where Kids Stay—and Play, and Eat—For Free

In this tough economy, there are hotels and resorts where you can go, stay, eat, and play for minimal dollars, and sometimes even for free.

You probably already know that at many hotel chains, kids under 18 can stay in a room with their parents for free. That's assuming the room has two double beds—one for the parents and one for the kids—or else you're looking at paying for a cot.

But when it comes to actual money-saving deals, look toward very traditional vacation destinations that desperately need the business. Mexico and the Caribbean, ski resorts, and cruise lines are practically falling over themselves to entice the visitors who need great value: families.

Various **Club Med** properties frequently feature discount programs such as Kids Stay Free and Half Off Your Better Half. With the first one, kids ages 15 and younger stay for free on a 7-night vacation with a paying adult—which means that your child is eating, drinking, sleeping, and playing for free. A sample 7-night stay at the Club Med Cancún Yucatán in late March without that promotion would cost just over $6,000.00 for two adults and two kids; with the promotion, you're looking at about $5,000 for all four people, or about $178.00 per person per night, including all of your meals and drinks (including alcohol for the adults).

Here's an example of just how badly the resorts want your business. After major holidays like Christmas, New Year's, and President's Day, Club Med often offers 2-free-days promotions, but after Christmas 2008, it also threw in free airfare.

Another all-inclusive chain called **Occidental Hotels & Resorts** has four brands (Allegro, Occidental Grand, Royal Hideaway, and Occidental Hotels) throughout the Caribbean, Mexico, Costa Rica, the Dominican Republic, and Spain. Every year between May 1 and December 18, kids under age 12 stay for free. Of the bunch, Allegro has the most affordable resorts. So, for a week-long trip in late April 2009 for a family of four, you're talking

---

Tip: If your hotel or resort doesn't have a babysitting service, check out Sitter City. Although the site doesn't vet babysitters directly, it walks prospective employers through a four-step screening process, including a background check and a list of important questions to ask ahead of time. Babysitters who consistently score well are ranked high on search queries.

▶▶ www.sittercity.com

about $337.00 a night; just a few weeks later, in May, the rate drops to $204.00 a night—for four people, including food, drinks, and activities. Not a bad deal!

Some value-oriented resorts add kids-stay-free promotions on top of already discounted prices. **Jolly Beach Resort & Spa** properties in the Caribbean, for example, fall into the three-star category when compared with resorts like Club Med, but here, rates start around $140.00 per night per person, including all meals, and offers morning and evening supervised activities for kids and teens. And in the low seasons, the rates drop even more: Between mid-April and December 20, one child stays free and a second child between the ages of 3 and 11 stays for $56.00 a night. In that same period, single parents staying with two kids in a standard room aren't charged any single supplement fee.

> **Bottom line:** Family-oriented resorts know their audience, so look for recurring deals outside of the peak travel seasons. When you factor in food, drinks (including alcohol for the parents), and activities, you're going to get significant savings.

▶▶ Club Med, www.clubmed.com

▶▶ Occidental Hotels & Resorts, www.occidentalhotels.com

▶▶ Jolly Beach Resort & Spa, www.jollybeachresort.com

Ski Resorts

Ski resorts are also feeling the pain and will be particularly hard hit during the slow periods after Thanksgiving and New Year's. And this year, those lulls may extend well into the rest of the ski season.

In **Jackson Hole, Wyoming,** planes are now arriving with 20 percent of their seats empty. If that trend continues, the airlines will most likely reduce 20 percent of the available seats, and prices will inevitably rise.

Ski resorts are extremely sensitive to that scenario and have been pricing accordingly.

In the 2008–2009 season, **Steamboat, Colorado,** partnered with both United and American Airlines for a kids-fly-free promotion for midweek travel from early to mid-December and early January to mid-February. Even better, that deal could be bundled with other discounts like free skiing for kids 12 and under (with a 5-day or longer adult lift ticket), which would drop a family's price significantly. Without those packages, you're paying at least $42.00 a day for a kid's ski pass and a midweek airfare of about $250.00.

Telluride, Colorado, arranged for kids to fly from Chicago or Dallas on American Airlines for no charge as part of a 5-day package. That deal was good with arrival on Sunday through Wednesday from early January through mid-February, traditionally a dead period.

> **Bottom line:** Don't pay full price at a ski resort without first exploring all the options. Is staying an extra day going to get you free lift tickets? Will traveling midweek save you a couple hundred dollars? In many cases, the answer is yes. But you need to ask—it's not always advertised. And like just about everything else these days, prices can often be negotiated beyond the officially advertised rates—even on special deals.

▶▶ Jackson Hole, Wyoming, www.jacksonhole.com

▶▶ Steamboat, Colorado, www.steamboat.com

▶▶ Telluride, Colorado, www.telluride.com, www.tellurideskiresort.com

Cruises

When it comes to cruising, families tend to gravitate toward mid-level lines like **Royal Caribbean, Carnival, Norwegian,** and **Princess,** where there are amenities like babysitting services, supervised kids' and teens' clubs, rock-climbing walls, and ice-skating rinks.

Disney Cruise Line, of course, is chock-full of kid-friendly programming—and, in fact, is offering a kids-sail-free promotion on most 3-night *Disney Wonder* sailings through May 28,

2009, for kids 12 and under with two paying adults. And when you take into account that meals are included, you might even be saving money by taking your family on a cruise!

> **Bottom line:** Cruises are a great option for families because they give kids the opportunity to venture out on their own without straying too far from Mom and Dad. But watch out for the asterisks: Babysitting services will cost you about $8.00 an hour and may not include diaper duty; shore excursions are going to be an added expense; and even sodas cost extra.

▶▶ Royal Caribbean, www.royalcaribbean.com

▶▶ Carnival, www.carnival.com

▶▶ Norwegian Cruise Line, www.ncl.com

▶▶ Princess Cruises, www.princess.com

▶▶ Disney Cruise Line, www.disneycruise.com

> **Tip:** A great option for families—and you'd never guess this one—is to travel by rented recreational vehicle. RV sales may be down, which is why RV rentals have suddenly become very attractive. You get to pack in a lot more sightseeing along the way than you do with flying, and you'll meet other travelers in a way that isn't likely in a hotel.
>
> And then there are the savings: Renting a 31-foot C-class motor home for a week will run you about $1,500.00, including mileage and insurance. Add in about $35.00 for a night in an RV park, plus gasoline, and that price can jump closer to $2,000.00, which still breaks down to about $70.00 a day for a family of four. Factor in the savings from carrying your own luggage (rather than checking it in) and cooking your own meals, and the savings are even more significant.
>
> But, one big caution here: RV travel means you'll be spending a lot of quality time with your family. Know what you're getting into before committing to a 3-week national park driving tour with three generations crammed into a 31-foot vehicle with one bathroom, or you'll be looking at a Griswold-style family vacation from hell!

CHAPTER 7

TRAVEL DISCOUNTS YOU DIDN'T KNOW ABOUT

AT TIMES LIKE THESE, everyone doesn't just want a deal. Everyone *needs* a deal. And therein lies a big problem. What, exactly, constitutes a real deal? A real discount?

Sometimes, the actual deal is hidden in the semantics. Stay 3 nights and get the 4th night free, for example. Assuming you wanted to stay 4 nights, then you are the beneficiary of a 25 percent discount. Other "value added" deals—whether they're free meals, resort credits, free parking, or free lift tickets—can have real value. But again, the caveat is that value has real meaning only if you needed the value-added goodies in the first place.

Then there are the discounts that are based on being a member of an organization, being of a certain age (or beyond), or being a member of an affinity group. Here again, it gets down to a definition of terms. Is the discount against the full

> Tip: Even Sam's Club members can take advantage of travel discounts because of its partnership with Expedia.com. The bonus with booking through the Sam's Club Web site is that you still benefit from Expedia's "best price guarantee," so if you book a trip and then find a better price online for the exact same trip within 24 hours, Expedia will refund the difference. It's not worth getting a Sam's Club membership solely for the travel benefit, but it's a worthwhile perk if you're already a member.
>
> ▶▶ http://travel.samsclub.com

published rate, or is it a bona fide discount against the current lowest rate? It's a significant distinction that must be addressed, especially now.

What about existing corporate discounts? This is a slippery slope, because corporate discounts are often negotiated 6 months to a year out, and in many cases they represent a percentage off the highest published airfare, hotel room rate, or rental-car tariff. In the mercurial world of fluctuating fares, it is not unusual for you to be able to significantly beat that corporate rate on your own, especially when fares are dropping across the board.

Perhaps the most important piece of advice I can give is that even when you get to a mutually agreeable definition of terms, there's still room to maneuver. In a serious buyers' market, not only is everything for sale, even the discounted prices are often negotiable. That's why it's crucial that you don't just opt for the first discount you qualify for, but instead explore all options— and then talk to a human being to see if you can do even better.

Let's start with senior discounts.

Senior

Don't expect any love from the airlines these days. Senior discounts on airlines have gone the way of the dodo. However, **Southwest Airlines** offers a limited number of Senior Fare tickets on each flight for travelers ages 65 and older. That means advance purchase isn't required, and tickets are refundable and changeable. But don't choose the senior discount immediately. Do your research and chances are you'll find a price on this budget carrier that's even cheaper than the senior fare.

Trains

Amtrak's senior-citizen discount gets travelers 62 years of age and older 15 percent off the lowest available rail fare on "most" trains. That doesn't include the Auto Train or the weekday Acela Express, and it's applicable only to coach fares. Services that are operated jointly by Amtrak and **VIA Rail Canada** offer a 10 percent discount for travelers ages 60 and over.

Car Rentals
You'll find that most car-rental companies offer discounts for seniors, but if you have an AARP or **AAA** card, you can usually match or better those existing deals—sometimes getting as much as 25 percent off.

Hotels
Senior discounts from hotels are prevalent, but can be quite nominal—we're talking about 5 to 10 percent off. However, here's a tip: When making a hotel reservation—which means calling the property directly, *not* the toll-free number—don't automatically ask for the senior discount. Instead, ask for the best available

rate, and then ask for a senior discount on top of that. That way they can't inflate the base price before giving the discount.

Here are some chains that regularly offer better-than-average senior discounts.

- **Marriott** hotels (including **JW Marriott, Renaissance, Residence Inn, Fairfield Inn,** and **TownePlace Suites**) worldwide offer at least 15 percent savings for guests ages 62 years and older.
- **Choice Hotels** (which includes **Cambria Suites, Clarion, Comfort Inn, Comfort Suites, Econo Lodge, MainStay Suites, Quality Inn, Rodeway Inn, Sleep Inn,** and **Suburban Extended Stay**) offers only 10 percent savings for travelers ages 50 and older, but raises it to 20 to 30 percent for travelers ages 60 and older.
- **Hyatt Hotels and Resorts** offers travelers ages 62 and older up to 50 percent off the prevailing rates (i.e., the regular rates for the days you're staying) at participating hotels in the continental United States and Canada.

Cruising

Unfortunately, if there's one place you're probably not going to find senior discounts, it's on a cruise. Why? Because that's who's cruising! Cruise lines generally can't offer discounts until close to the departure date, when they're desperate to fill up cabins. And in that case, anyone can take advantage of deeply gouged prices, not just seniors.

Tip: If you are, or were, an educator, the Educators Bed and Breakfast Travel Network can save you money on your next travel experience. This peer network invites educators to host one another for nominal costs— about $40.00 a night for a room for two adults and any children under 18 years. An annual membership costs about $36.00.

▶▶ www.educatorstravel.com

Student

International Student Identity Cards

Students on a budget can save big with these cards, which offer travel discounts worldwide. **International Student Identity Cards (ISICs)** are available for full-time students ages 12 to 25. Benefits include free or discounted admission to major museums, 10 to 15 percent off at participating restaurants, up to 30 percent off select travel guides, 15 percent off Amtrak, 10 percent off at various hotels and hostels, 15 percent off passport expediting services, and much more. Like any discount card, its value depends on how much you use it, but at $22.00 a year, it seems like a no-brainer to me.

> **Tip:** Don't let your student ID card sit unused in your wallet. A student ID isn't good only for discounted movie tickets; it also gets you perks like free entrance to all national museums and national monuments in Athens, Greece, and 25 percent off shipping with Greyhound PackageXpress. It doesn't hurt to ask anywhere you're buying goods or services. You'll be surprised by how many establishments are willing to help their ramen-eating constituents.

If you're not a student, but you are between the ages of 12 and 25, the **International Youth Travel Card** is the way to go. It offers fewer discounts than the ISIC, but with up to 30 percent savings on guidebooks, half off entrance to museums, and access to free global SIM (Subscriber Identity Module) cards to make international calls, it is still worth the $22.00 annual price tag.

▶▶ International Student Identity Cards, www.isic.org

Student Advantage Discount Card

This card has a few travel benefits but is primarily geared toward college necessities like books, computers, and clothing. If you have one in your back pocket, great—you can get 15 percent off on Amtrak and Greyhound tickets, up to 20 percent off at Alamo Rent a Car, and even 10 percent off a "party boat" to the Bahamas with Discovery Cruise Line (parents, don't ask). But in some cases, you may not even need the card to get a discount—a quick call to Alamo dropped a $103.00-per-day car rental down to about $54.00 a day, based on a list of universities whose students automatically get discounts if they can show ID upon arrival. So, don't purchase this $20.00 card for the sole purpose of saving travel dollars.

Military
Airlines

It took something bordering on a scandal, but most airlines have finally waived the second- or third-checked-bag fee for our nation's military members. In the summer of 2008, an Army National Guard soldier complained that American Airlines had charged him $100.00 for a third checked bag that was filled with military equipment. To be fair, checked-bag fees for our men and women in uniform are supposed to be reimbursed by the government, but adding even that layer of red tape to the travel of our country's finest sparked outrage. Soon after, American waived the third-bag fee for all military; Continental followed suit, and Delta took it a step further by waiving all checked-bag fees.

Space-A Flights

You may have heard of something called space-available flights, a.k.a. Space-A flights or military hops. With this status, military personnel—current and retired service members and their families—can travel for next to nothing by filling up empty seats on military aircraft. However, since 9/11, this has become nearly impossible to plan in advance. Mission schedules used to be posted on the Web, and travelers could even sign up for spots online—but that has been discontinued. Instead, passengers must register in person or via fax or e-mail at the specific passenger terminals located at US Air Force airfields (check out www.baseops.net/spaceatravel for a list of terminals worldwide). But remember, even if you get on a flight, this isn't a terribly reliable method of transportation. First, it can take months before a spot even opens up, and you may not be notified that you have a seat until the day of departure. And, if you do get seated and your aircraft stops to pick up official-duty passengers or cargo, you can get bumped right off the plane!

When it comes to regular airlines, discounted military airfares aren't a hard-and-fast rule, but some special offers are out there. For example, **American Airlines** frequently offers discounts for active-duty members who are on leave or furlough—but there's no standard, across-the-board discount. It just means that special fares are available on certain routes, they probably have more flexibility than other discounted fares, and they're available only when booking over the phone.

Like any other special fare, it's best to shop around to see if you can beat it on your own. For example, a recently advertised military fare on American Airlines was $109.00 each way for Dallas-Fort Worth to New Orleans, not including taxes and fees, through December 31, 2008. A quick search of American's Web site showed the same route available for a regular round-trip price of $203.00 ($224.00 with taxes and fees)—pretty much the same deal as the advertised military fare.

> Tip: Check resources like www.military.com to find deals created exclusively for members of the US Armed Forces.

Trains

Active-duty US military personnel and their families can get 10 percent off the lowest fare on most Amtrak trains. This applies only to coach travel and doesn't include travel on certain Amtrak Thruway connecting services or Canadian portions operated jointly by Amtrak and VIA Rail Canada. Bottom line? You can save just as much with a AAA membership, but if you have a US Armed Forces ID card, it's worth showing it at the ticket counter.

Hotels

Though it's not well advertised, hotels will often cut their rates for military personnel. At most major hotel chains, you just have to ask for a government rate, which is based on a specified Federal Per Diem (a guaranteed rate based on the federal government's assessment of how much military personnel receive for lodging). Check out www.hotelsatperdiem.com for General Service Administration–approved hotels that always have a government rate that is at or below the Federal Per Diem rate for their location. Find out the official per diem at www.gsa.gov.

Choice Hotels recently launched the **Choice Privileges Armed Services** program in partnership with the US military. Active, reserve, and retired military, National Guard, and Coast Guard members and their families automatically get Elite Gold status in the chain's frequent-stay program. So that means you earn additional points that can be redeemed for free hotel stays worldwide with no blackout dates; airline rewards; and special hotel privileges such as express check-in, late checkout, and free Internet.

Car Rentals

Like hotels, most car-rental agencies offer government rates to government officials and military personnel. However, unlike lodging and meals, renting a car is not a per diem expense—it's a separate transportation expense. Under the US Government Car Rental Agreement, participating car-rental companies provide benefits such as free collision/liability damage waiver insurance, no fees for additional or underage drivers, free unlimited mileage, and "highly competitive" rates. Translation? You may very well beat whatever deal they come up with on your own, but it's worth comparing options.

Tip: Are travel club memberships worth it? Yes, if you like to travel in groups and plan to travel more than once a year. The Bloomfield, New Jersey–based Women's Travel Club and its parent company, Club ABC Tours, charge $30.00 a year (or $45.00 for 2 years) and, in exchange, members can participate in group trips. The pitch is that by having a built-in network of travelers, organizers can negotiate deeper discounts with group bulk rates, so you get access to deals the average Web surfer doesn't. And in the case of a women's travel club (Club ABC has them for senior, solo, and high-roller travelers, too), it's more likely that you'll be surrounded by like-minded individuals and, therefore, you'll have better travel experience.

▶▶ Women's Travel Club, www.womenstravelclub.com

▶▶ Club ABC Tours, www.clubabc.com

CHAPTER 8

ONE-TANK TRIPS

IN THE MERCURIAL WORLD of oil prices, there are no guarantees. Nothing is certain except our addiction to oil and . . . uncertainty. And there is one more truth: No matter what the price of oil is, we will still find a way to travel. We adjust.

Memorial Day 2008. Major media outlets reported that, according to AAA, there would be fewer Americans on the road because of the high gas prices. It seemed like a reasonable, logical assumption.

But was it? What metric did AAA use to come to that apparently conclusive prediction? The answer: They projected the number of cars that would be on the road.

And that was the linchpin of its flawed analysis and failure to acknowledge the reality of how Americans adjust to crisis.

Yes, AAA counted the number of cars on the road. But did it count the number of people in those cars? Memorial Day was, in essence, a continuous convoy of the *Beverly Hillbillies'* Clampett family, all crammed into the family sedan, except for Granny, who was sitting in a rocking chair strapped to the roof.

Yes, there may have been fewer cars on the road, but there weren't fewer people. When it came to travel, we had simply—and quickly—adjusted.

Whether oil prices stabilize or continue their wild roller-coaster ride is more or less immaterial to the core seductions that drive us—sometimes literally. And in the case of travel by automobile, we continue to adjust, and we continue to travel.

But now, we're doing it more creatively and more efficiently. Hence the evolution of the one-tank trip: an opportunity to travel on great routes and itineraries while having great experiences . . . on one tank of gas.

Here are some of my favorite itineraries.

One-way calculations are based on gasoline costs of $2.50 per gallon, a 25-mpg car, and no significant traffic. Cost of gas is based on a vehicle with a 14-gallon tank traveling from destination to destination with no detours. Routes are approximations and should not be used in place of a map.

Arizona
Phoenix to Flagstaff

Distance: 145 miles
Time: 2 hours, 11 minutes
Gas: $14.50
Route: I-17 North to AZ-89

Flagstaff is perhaps best known as a lively college town, but it hosts more than just fraternity parties. Nearby national monuments, museums, and vast playgrounds for hikers, bikers, and skiers attract year-round visitors. Once you arrive, ditch the car and hop on public transportation to get around. The $3.00 day pass on the **Mountain Line** buses is a deal compared with paying $1.00 per one-way trip. The 32-run **Arizona Snowbowl** ($49.00 for an adult 1-day pass) is a top skiing destination, but head to the **Coconino National Forest's Red Mountain** or **Humphreys Peak Trail** in the off-season for scenic hiking and biking. **Heritage Square** offers free summer concerts every weekend at 2:00 p.m.

▶▶ Mountain Line, www.mountainline.az.gov

▶▶ Arizona Snowbowl, www.arizonasnowbowl.com

▶▶ Coconino National Forest, www.fs.fed.us/r3/coconino

▶▶ Heritage Square, www.heritagesquaretrust.org

On the way . . . Scottsdale

Less than 20 miles northeast of Phoenix is Scottsdale. With a pro-liferation of boutique hotels, art galleries (more than 100 in the city center alone), and plenty of bars, Scottsdale has grown from a sleepy Southwest town to a trendy destination. Check out the **Scottsdale Museum of Contemporary Art** ($7.00 for admission), where you'll find art genres different from the majority of south-western styles you'll see elsewhere around town. And you can't miss the 20th-century buildings of **Old Town**, Scottsdale's popular shopping district. Architect Frank Lloyd Wright lived in the city, so locals pay homage to him by preserving landmarks such as his mid-20th-century abode, **Taliesen West** (adult tours start at $32).

▶▶ Scottsdale Museum of Contemporary Art, www.smoca.org

▶▶ Old Town, www.scottsdaledowntown.com

▶▶ Taliesen West, www.franklloydwright.org

Sedona

Just south of Flagstaff, off AZ-17, Sedona has inspired poets, artists, and travel writers galore with its natural red-rock scenery, which literally glows at sunset. For the best views, head to **Cathe-dral Rock** at dusk or to **Airport Mesa,** which also happens to be one of the best-known energy vortexes in the world. That's right, the discovery of Sedona's energy "vortexes" in the 1980s led to the city's rebirth as a healing retreat. New Age believers flock to Sedona from around the world, and you'll be bombarded with this concept as soon as you step into town. While the city has its fair share of charmless strip malls, there are still plenty of favorite local spots, like ancient Indian ruins and **Slide Rock** park, now a state park with a popular swimming hole. Before you go, get your free Sedona guide from www.visitsedona.com.

▶▶ Cathedral Rock, www.wildsedona.com/trails/cathedral.htm

▶▶ Slide Rock State Park, www.azstateparks.com/Parks/SLRO

Tucson to Nogales, Arizona, and Nogales, Sonora, Mexico

Distance: 66.2 miles
Time: 1 hour, 6 minutes
Gas: $6.62
Route: I-19 South to AZ-189/West Mariposa Road

It may be a short drive from Tucson to Nogales, Arizona, but don't forget your passport! Arizona's largest US-Mexico border town has close ties to its neighbor of the same name, Nogales, Sonora. Drive to **Crawford Street,** where there are multiple parking lots that cost less than $5.00 a day, and you'll be 2 blocks from the border. On foot, head straight to the shopping center in downtown Nogales, Sonora, for inexpensive and handmade rugs, pottery, and crafts. If you decide to drive into Mexico, Nogales is part of the "free circulation zone," which means you don't need a vehicle permit. However, to travel outside of the free zone, you'll need to obtain a free decal at the "kilometer 98" checkpoint on AZ-15.

▶▶ Nogales-Santa Cruz County Chamber of Commerce,
www.thenogaleschamber.com

▶▶ Sonora Tourism, www.gotosonora.com

▶▶ US Customs and Border Protection Nogales Service Port, 520-287-1410

On the way . . . Patagonia

Instead of driving the straight shot between Tucson and Nogales, take the scenic route on I-10 to the Sonoita Highway (AZ-83) so you can stop in Patagonia—a haven for outdoor enthusiasts with its state parks; preserves; and hiking, biking, and horseback riding trails. For example, the **Arizona Trail,** which runs for 800 miles from Mexico to Utah, runs right through the city. The Nature Conservancy's **Patagonia-Sonoita Creek Preserve** ($5.00 admission for nonmembers) boasts nearly 300 species of birds.

For a quirky family experience, visit **Square Top Ranch,** where you can see a herd of 15 to 20 alpacas at any given time. And, if you're a history buff, don't miss the many ghost towns located within an hour's drive; these date back to the city's mining era: Harshaw, Duquesne, Mowry, Lochiel, and Washington Camp.

▶▶ Arizona Trail, www.aztrail.org

▶▶ Patagonia-Sonoita Creek Preserve, www.nature.org/wherewework/ northamerica/states/arizona/preserves/art1972.html

▶▶ Square Top Ranch, www.squaretopranch.com

Arizona Vineyards Winery

As you're driving south on the Patagonia Highway to Nogales, stop by **Arizona Vineyards.** Even though the state isn't known as a wine destination, this 25-year-old establishment is considered to be a top-tier tasting room, and it offers free wine tastings daily. Try the Rattlesnake Red, Desert Dust, Apache Red, and Coyote Red wines—named appropriately for their Southwestern home.

▶▶ Arizona Vineyards, 520-287-7972

California
San Francisco to Mendocino

Distance: 154 miles
Time: 3 hours, 14 minutes
Gas: $15.40
Route: US-101 North to CA-128 West to CA-1

Only about 1,000 residents live in Mendocino year-round, but in the summer months, this oceanside town is booming. With the Pacific Ocean, redwood trees, and vineyards all within a few miles of one another, this is a true California experience. Mendocino has long been an artist's haven, so start at the **Mendocino**

Art Center (free admission), where you can mosey around the galleries, shops, and gardens.

> Tip: Check out the free artist receptions on the second Saturday evening of each month at the Mendocino Art Center.

If you have a sweet tooth, head to **Mendocino Jams and Preserves.** Their treats are made from locally grown fruits, so it's worth splurging the few dollars for a jar—take advantage of the free samples to find your favorite. Residents frequent **Mendocino Headlands State Park** for hiking, jogging, and general sightseeing. It's situated beside the ocean, surrounding downtown Mendocino. In the winter, whale sightings are frequent, but do as the locals do and keep your distance from the unforgiving cliffs near the water.

▶▶ Mendocino Art Center, www.mendocinoartcenter.org

▶▶ Mendocino Jams and Preserves, 707-937-1037

▶▶ Mendocino Headlands State Park, www.parks.ca.gov

On the way . . . Sausalito

Sausalito is an expensive final destination, but it's a beautiful stop for lunch or a stroll. The town of only 8,000 is situated by the ocean and is easily navigable on foot. Either pop right over the Golden Gate Bridge from San Francisco or take a half-hour ride on the **Golden Gate Ferry** ($7.45 for an adult one-way), which runs frequently between San Francisco and Sausalito. Sneak away from the main strip on Bridgeway to **Caledonia Street,** where you'll find less-crowded restaurants and galleries. The **Sausalito Art Festival** takes place every Labor Day weekend, attracting nearly 50,000 people and showcasing more than 20,000 original works of art. The US Army Corps of Engineers'

Bay Model Visitor Center ($3.00 donation) is a sight worth seeing if you stop by while the 1½-acre model of the San Francisco Bay is operating.

▶▶ Golden Gate Ferry Service, www.goldengateferry.org

▶▶ Sausalito Art Festival, www.sausalitoartfestival.org

▶▶ Bay Model Visitor Center, www.spn.usace.army.mil/bmvc

Santa Rosa

Tourist brochures will tell you to visit the town of Healdsburg on your drive through Sonoma County's wine country, but don't skip over neighboring Santa Rosa, a major transportation hub in the early 1900s. First visit **Historic Railroad Square,** which plays host to local restaurants and boutique shops. *Peanuts* fans can't miss the **Charles M. Schulz Museum and Research Center,** which showcases the work of the famous cartoonist and offers cartooning classes and other workshops ($8.00 admission, $25.00 for classes). And then, of course, get some wine: **Benzinger Family Winery** (tastings start at $10.00) has been around since the 1980s and offers tram tours of the winery and vineyard. Chocolate lovers are also in for a treat: **Wine Country Chocolates** has the Sonoma Valley's first chocolate-tasting room, which features handmade delicacies like wine-filled truffles.

▶▶ Historic Railroad Square, www.railroadsquare.net

▶▶ Charles M. Schulz Museum and Research Center,
www.schulzmuseum.org

▶▶ Santa Rosa Food and Wine, www.tastesantarosa.com

▶▶ Benzinger Family Winery, www.benziger.com

▶▶ Wine Country Chocolates, www.winecountrychocolates.com

Los Angeles to Santa Barbara County's Wine Country

Distance: 124 miles
Time: 2 hours, 19 minutes
Cost: $12.40
Route: US-101 North to Exit 139, Santa Rosa Road

California wine country isn't only about Napa and Sonoma. Southern California's Santa Barbara Wine Country is made up of half a dozen regions that produce some of the best local wines. You'll have options for spas, shopping, and, of course, wine tasting. Check in with the Santa Barbara County Vintners' Association for a list of wineries, vineyards, and driving routes.

▶▶ Santa Barbara County Vintners' Association, www.sbcountywines.com

On the way . . . Buellton and Lompoc

Two prestigious tasting rooms in this county are at **Babcock Winery and Vineyards** ($10.00 tasting) and **Melville Vineyards and Winery** ($10.00 tasting), both in Lompoc. Also visit **Casa Cassara** ($8.00 tasting) in Buellton, an exclusive, 2,500-case winery that hosts festivals, tasting events, even concerts. Make time for dinner at **Pea Soup Andersen's**, a Buellton favorite. And, if you're an ostrich egg fan (and who isn't?), don't miss **OstrichLand USA** ($4.00 admission) in Buellton, where you can stock up on free-range ostrich eggs.

▶▶ Babcock Winery and Vineyards, www.babcockwinery.com

▶▶ Melville Vineyards and Winery, www.melvillewinery.com

▶▶ Casa Cassara Winery and Vineyard, www.casacassarawinery.com

▶▶ Pea Soup Andersen's, www.peasoupandersens.net

▶▶ OstrichLand USA, www.ostrichlandusa.com

Los Olivos

This small town is packed with tasting rooms, art galleries, pricey boutiques, and epicurean restaurants, but deals are to be found here.

Brave the lunch lines at **Panino,** where locals come back for the delicious and inexpensive sandwiches. **Mattei's Tavern** at the edge of town has been serving brews since it was built as a stagecoach stop in 1886. For a splurge, drive further along CA-154 to **Los Olivos Grocery,** a favorite for hard-to-find cheeses, local organic produce, gelato, and a vast selection of spices, oils, and, of course, wines.

▶▶ Panino, www.paninorestaurants.com

▶▶ Mattei's Tavern, www.matteistavern.com

▶▶ Los Olivos Grocery, www.losolivosgrocery.com

San Diego to Yuma, Arizona

Distance: 172 miles
Time: 2 hours, 36 minutes
Gas: $17.20
Route: I-8 East to Exit 172, Winterhaven Drive

If you thought San Diego was the land of sunshine, try driving to Yuma, Arizona, where the sun shines 91 percent of the year, making it the sunniest place on earth, according to Guinness World Records. It's also where 90 percent of the country's winter vegetables grow, which is why the annual **Yuma Lettuce Days Festival** isn't out of place. Every January, you have the chance to purchase top-quality produce and take a free bus tour of Yuma's agricultural fields. The **Yuma River Daze Arts and Crafts Festival** is another festival that occurs every February, with more than 100 booths of local art, music, and food. Golf lovers should hit the **Desert Hills Golf Course** (greens fees start at $28.00), which is a par-72 championship course. The best time to visit Yuma is when the rest of the country is cold; by late spring, it gets too hot to spend much time outdoors.

▶▶ Lettuce Days Festival, www.yumaheritage.com

▶▶ Desert Hills Golf Course, www.deserthillsgc.com

On the way . . . Felicity

Just before you reach Yuma, you may find yourself in a town called Felicity. If you've ever wanted to claim you've been to the center of the world, don't miss this stop. The town was given that title by author Jacques-Andres Istel in a 1985 children's book and it was enacted into law shortly thereafter. The locale embraces its claim to fame by hosting a pyramid that is allegedly at the world's center. Tours are available from Thanksgiving to Easter.

▶▶ Felicity, www.felicityusa.com

Los Algodones, Mexico

South of the border from Yuma is a tiny Mexican town called Los Algodones. What makes this place so special? Low-cost dental work! That's right, in this town of about 15,000, there are at least 350 dentists and 50 pharmacies, and you can get high-quality dental work done for up to 60 percent less than in the United States. Don't worry, most of these dentists were actually trained in the United States. Just park for about $7.00 on the US side and walk one block to cross the border.

▶▶ Los Algodones, www.losalgodones.com

Colorado
Denver to Georgetown

> Distance: 48 miles
> Time: 49 minutes
> Gas: $4.80
> Route: I-70 West to Exit 228

Since the Gold Rush made Colorado what it is today, it's worth traveling around the "Gold Circle" towns of Georgetown, Golden, and Idaho Springs. Due west of Denver is Georgetown, your final stop on the Gold Circle route. Hit the main commercial strip, **Sixth Street,** for antiques shopping and local markets housed in buildings that are, for the most part, circa the 1800s. Even if you can't stay the night, check out the restaurant and occasional wine dinners at the **Peck House,** the oldest operating hotel in Colorado. For a scenic tour of the area, take a train ride along the **Royal Gorge Route** (starting at $32.95 for adults).

▶▶ Peck House, www.thepeckhouse.com

▶▶ Royal Gorge Route, www.royalgorgeroute.com

On the way . . . Golden

This aptly named traditional Gold Rush town is located just north of the highway between Denver and Georgetown. Once you're there, take free public tours of the historic district and the **MillerCoors** brewery (hang around for the free tastings). Then, explore Colorado's Wild Wild West with a visit to the **Buffalo Bill Museum and Grave** ($3.00 admission), which contains memorabilia from the Pony Express and his Wild West Show. Golden's don't-miss burger joint is the **Old Capital Grill,** so make that a stop for lunch or dinner.

▶▶ MillerCoors brewery, www.millercoors.com

▶▶ Buffalo Bill Museum and Grave, www.buffalobill.org

▶▶ Old Capital Grill, 303-279-6390

Idaho Springs

Who said the mining days are over? You'll pass through this old gold-mining town en route from Golden to Georgetown. While you're there, check out the **Argo Gold Mine and Mill** ($15.00 admission), where you can pan for gold and gemstones, and keep your finds. Also, take a tour of the gold mine, which has barely changed since the 1800s, and the museum. The Victorian downtown of Idaho Springs is home to the largest waterwheel in Colorado, the **Charlie Taylor Water Wheel.** If you're craving mountain pizza, grab a slice at the famous **Beau Jo's Colorado Style Pizza**.

▶▶ Argo Gold Mine, Mill, and Museum, www.historicargotours.com

▶▶ Beau Jo's Colorado Style Pizza, www.beaujos.com

Florida
Miami to Key West

Distance: 160 miles
Time: 3 hours, 32 minutes
Gas: $16.00
Route: I-95 South to FL-874 South to FL-821 South to US-1
South

The first thing you should know about the drive to Key West is this: There's traffic. The drive itself can make or break your trip, so be sure to check out traffic reports before you hit the road. Once you do reach Key West, head to the **Ernest Hemingway Home and Museum** ($12.00 admission) to learn about the author's life and admire the 60-plus cats on-site (paying homage to the author's feline fetish). Though it may be a tourist trap, you can't leave the island without a trip to **Sloppy Joe's,** which has been open since 1937. A traditional Sloppy Joe sandwich will set you back $8.50. If you head to Duval Street for shopping, consider renting mopeds or bikes from a company like **The Moped Hospital** to get around (about $35.00 per day).

▶▶ Ernest Hemingway Home, www.hemingwayhome.com

▶▶ Sloppy Joe's, www.sloppyjoes.com

▶▶ The Moped Hospital, www.mopedhospital.com

On the way . . . Key Largo
Fishing enthusiasts flock to Key Largo for the perfect catch. Divers embrace Largo's reefs and underwater scenery. You can

enjoy the solace provided by **John Pennekamp Coral Reef State Park,** the first underwater state park in the country. Also check out the plethora of art galleries, like the aptly named **Key Largo Art Gallery,** that feature inexpensive and locally inspired works. Whatever the water sport, **Caribbean Watersports** can provide rental equipment throughout the Keys—be it a kayak, paddleboat, or personal motorized watercraft.

▶▶ John Pennekamp Coral Reef State Park, www.pennekamppark.com

▶▶ Key Largo Art Gallery, www.keylargoartgallery.com

▶▶ Caribbean Watersports, www.caribbeanwatersports.com

Orlando to Florida's Space Coast, Orsino

Distance: 53.6 miles
Time: 1 hour, 2 minutes
Gas: $5.36
Route: FL-408 East to FL-417 South to FL-528 East to I-95 South to Exit 195, Fiske Boulevard

Drive east from Orlando toward the coast and . . . three, two, one, blast off! The Space Coast is best known for the **Kennedy Space Center** ($38.00 admission).

But even if you're not a space geek, there are plenty of other—affordable—activities available in this area. **Space Coast Stadium** is home to the minor-league Brevard County Manatees and spring-training games for the major league Washington Nationals ($5.00 to $20.00 per ticket). And don't forget to check out Port Canaveral's three public beaches—**Jetty Park** ($5.00 per car), **Rodney S. Ketcham Park,** and **Freddie Patrick Park** (both free)—for swimming, surfing, fishing, and bird-watching.

▶▶ Kennedy Space Center, www.kennedyspacecenter.com

▶▶ Minor League Baseball schedule, www.minorleaguebaseball.com

▶▶ Port Canaveral beaches, www.portcanaveral.org/recreation/beaches.php

On the way . . . Cocoa Beach

Farther down the coast is Cocoa Beach, a.k.a. the Jewel of the Space Coast. The **Cocoa Beach Surf Museum** chronicles 60 years of surfing with a wooden paddleboard from the 1940s, a collection of 1960s surfing art and music, and vintage surfing magazines. Afterward, put your knowledge to use with a lesson at the **Ron Jon Surf School** (lessons start at $45.00), or save a few dollars and take a guided nature tour along the Indian River Lagoon with **Cocoa Beach Kayaking** ($30.00). Keep your eyes open—you might spot dolphins and manatees.

▸▸ Cocoa Beach Surf Museum, www.cocoabeachsurfmuseum.org

▸▸ Ron Jon Surf School, www.ronjonsurfschool.com

▸▸ Cocoa Beach Kayaking, www.cocoabeachkayaking.com

Georgia
Atlanta to Athens

Distance: 74.3 miles
Time: 1 hour, 31 minutes
Gas: $7.43
Route: I-85 North to GA-316 East to US-29 North to Exit 7, College Station Road

Go, Bulldogs! Athens is home to the University of Georgia, and during football season, that won't be hard to tell. See the **Georgia Dogs** sports teams live during their respective seasons year-round, or head over to the campus to check out its extensive gardens or to catch an art show. Off campus, explore Athens's segment of the 100-mile **Antebellum Trail**. The town was one of the seven communities that escaped being destroyed by fire during Sherman's March in 1864. Take a stroll on **Clayton Street,** where you'll find plenty of eateries, art galleries, and shopping. And don't forget the town's music scene. The home of popular bands like R.E.M. and the B-52s, Athens never has a shortage of live music and memorabilia. Visit www.flagpole.com for an updated local music directory.

▶▶ Georgia Dogs, www.georgiadogs.com

▶▶ Antebellum Trail, www.historicgeorgia.com

On the way . . . Duluth

Take a short detour north off I-85 to the small southern town of Duluth. Art lovers should stop by **Carter House Gallery and Framing,** which specializes in traditional and contemporary pieces as well as custom framing, so you can look forward to displaying any finds upon your arrival home. Railroad buffs should also check out Georgia's official transportation-history museum, the **Southeastern Railway Museum** ($8.00 admission). Check out the collection of Georgia train memorabilia, including classic Pullman cars and steam locomotives; ride on restored cabooses; and tour the train car that helped "bring the Olympics to Atlanta" in 1996.

▶▶ Carter House Gallery and Framing, 770-495-1998

▶▶ Southeastern Railway Museum, www.srmduluth.org

Three Sisters Vineyards and Winery

If you get a craving for wine on your Georgia trek, drive north from Duluth on US-19 for about an hour until you hit Dahlonega, home to **Three Sisters Vineyards and Winery.** This small, family-run establishment has 18 acres of grapes and is open to the public from February to Christmas with free wine tastings. Or, choose a specialty tasting that starts at $10.00 per person, including the can't-miss wine-and-chocolate tasting.

▶▶ Three Sisters Vineyards, www.threesistersvineyards.com

Illinois
Chicago to Milwaukee

Distance: 92 miles
Time: 1 hour, 42 minutes
Gas: $9.20
Route: Edens Expressway West/I-94 West to I-43 North

If you're a beer drinker and motorcycle rider, you can't go wrong driving north from Chicago to Milwaukee. Wisconsin's largest city is home to the **Harley Davidson Museum** ($16.00 admission) and the **MillerCoors Milwaukee Brewery** (free). If you're on the beer circuit, continue on to the **Captain Frederick Pabst Mansion** ($8.00 admission). Built in 1892, Pabst's 37-room mansion was saved from demolition in 1975. Fortunately for non-beer-drinking nonmotor-cyclists, the city also plays host to a slew of museums and rare sights, including the relocated 15th-century French **Saint Joan of Arc Chapel** (free), believed to be the only functioning medieval building in the Western Hemisphere, and the **Annunciation Greek Orthodox Church** (free), one of Frank Lloyd Wright's final projects.

▶▶ Harley Davidson Museum, www.harley-davidson.com

▶▶ MillerCoors Milwaukee Brewery, www.millercoors.com

▶▶ Captain Frederick Pabst Mansion, www.pabstmansion.com

▶▶ Saint Joan of Arc Chapel, www.marquette.edu/chapel

▶▶ Annunciation Greek Orthodox Church, www.annunciationwi.com

On the way . . . Madison

You can drive a loop by heading northwest from Chicago to Madison, then driving east to Milwaukee. Wisconsin's state capitol sits between two lakes and is home to 40,000 college students and plenty of culture. Take the hourlong **State Street Walking Tour** ($5.00) for some local insight into the city's architecture and history. Downtown's **Capitol Square** is a must for great shopping and eating. On Wednesday and Saturday mornings, the square is home to an open-air market featuring fresh produce, handmade crafts, and local musicians. If you're craving the great outdoors, the **University of Wisconsin–Madison Arboretum** (free) is the place to go. The 1,200-acre terrain is vast and diverse—with prairies, savannas, hardwood forests, evergreen forests, marshes, and ponds.

▶▶ State Street Walking Tour, www.madisontrust.org

▶▶ University of Wisconsin–Madison Arboretum, www.uwarboretum.org

Illinois Beach State Park

On your way back down from Milwaukee to Chicago, stop at this quintessential state park that is always a nice retreat from city life. Situated on Lake Michigan, this unique park includes a beach in addition to plenty of hiking and biking trails. Cross-country skiing is popular in the winter, and lake swimming is all the rage in the summer.

▶▶ Illinois Beach State Park, www.dnr.state.il.us

Massachusetts
Boston to Lenox

Distance: 130 miles
Time: 2 hours, 30 minutes
Gas: $13.00
Route: I-90 West to US-20 West to MA-183 to Walker Street

Music lovers flock to Lenox every summer to catch the **Boston Symphony Orchestra** in its annual summer home. You can also see a show at **Shakespeare and Company** (tickets start at $10.00), which has year-round performances and a well-known fall festival. For a more spiritual musical experience, stop by one of the country's oldest churches, the **Church on the Hill**. This national landmark, open since 1770, hosts crafts fairs and $15.00 concerts year-round. American author Edith Wharton was a Lenox resident, and you can visit her home, the **Mount Estate and Gardens** ($10.00 admission for adults), which she created from the ground up and is a piece of art in itself. Take a tour through the mansion and its gardens anytime from May through October.

▶▶ Boston Symphony Orchestra, www.bso.org

▶▶ Shakespeare and Company, www.shakespeare.org

▶▶ Church on the Hill, www.churchonthehilllenox.org

▶▶ Mount Estate and Gardens, www.edithwharton.org

On the way . . . Cambridge

Cambridge is probably best known for its Ivy League resident, Harvard University. Even if you're not planning to apply, take a stroll through the campus with **Unofficial Tours** (free, but tips are highly encouraged), a company founded by former students who tell the "real" stories and anecdotes that go way beyond what's in the university handbook. Cambridge is a must for bookworms; there are more than 30 bookstores within a 6-mile radius, making it the city with the most bookstores per capita. In particular, check out **Rodney's Bookstore**, a 6,000-square-foot shop carrying everything from rare editions to best-sellers. If you want to include some theater or dance in your trip, your best bets are the **American Repertory Theatre** and the art galleries and dance and theater performances at Harvard (starting at $12.00) and the nearby Massachusetts Institute of Technology.

▶▶ Unofficial Tours, www.harvardtour.com

▶▶ Rodney's Bookstore, www.rodneysbookstore.com

▶▶ American Repertory Theatre, www.amrep.org

▶▶ Harvard Arts, www.harvard.edu/arts

▶▶ MIT Arts Calendar, http://artscal.mit.edu

Michigan
Detroit to Stratford, Ontario, Canada

Distance: 151 miles
Time: 2 hours, 51 minutes
Gas: $15.10
Route: I-94 East to Provincial Route 402 East to County
Road 81/Center Road to Elginfield Road to Highway 119/
County Road 7

Can you hear people speaking in iambic pentameter? If so, you
must be in Stratford, Ontario, located northeast (and a world
away) from Detroit. This little Canadian town is known for the
annual **Stratford Shakespeare Festival,** which showcases the works
of Shakespeare and other classics from April through October.
Stratford is also known for its art galleries, boutiques, and great
architecture, which dates back to 1832, when the city was founded.
From June through September, check out **Art in the Park,** an outdoor "museum" that features jury-selected artists on Wednesdays,
Saturdays, and Sundays. Free, 90-minute tours of the town are
available from the Visitor's Information Center, May to October.

▶▶ Stratford Festival, www.stratfordfestival.ca

▶▶ Art in the Park, www.artintheparkstratford.com

▶▶ Visitor's Information Center, www.welcometostratford.com

On the way . . . London, Ontario, Canada
Is a trip across the pond too much of a stretch on the wallet this
year? That's okay! In London, Ontario, you'll feel like you are in the

Queen's presence. Hop off Highway 402 and get into the British spirit by visiting the **Labatt Brewery** ($5.00 admission) and taking a tour of the site, which includes a free tasting. Festivals abound year-round in this small Canadian town, including the July **Bluesfest London** and **Rock the Park,** a classic-rock concert event.

▶▶ Labatt Brewery, www.labatt.com

▶▶ Bluesfest London, www.thebluesfest.com

▶▶ Rock the Park, www.rockthepark.ca

Minnesota
Minneapolis to Duluth

Distance: 154 miles
Time: 2 hours, 24 minutes
Gas: $15.40
Route: I-35 North to Exit 256B, Lake Avenue/5th Avenue West

Just drive northeast until you see water. Situated on the western shore of Lake Superior, Duluth is a true maritime town and home to the nation's only freshwater aquarium, the **Great Lakes Aquarium. Canal Park** is a great stop for local eats and shops, and for some local shipwreck history, go to the **Lake Superior Maritime Museum** (free). Be sure to take a stroll along Lakewalk to admire the lake and the city's landscape. Don't miss the **North Shore Scenic Drive** along Lake Superior, which stretches 154 miles from Duluth to Grand Portage.

▶▶ Great Lakes Aquarium, www.glaquarium.org

▶▶ Canal Park, www.canalparkduluth.com

▶▶ Lake Superior Maritime Museum, www.lsmma.com

▶▶ North Shore Scenic Drive, www.superiorbyways.com/north-shore-scenic-drive

On the way . . . Banning State Park

If wildlife is your thing, you won't tire of this state park, which boasts 184 bird species, 17 species of reptiles and amphibians, and 34 mammal species. Located along MN-23 near Sandstone, this park is home to a plethora of fox and deer, but beware of the black bears. For kayaking enthusiasts, **Hell's Gate Rapids** and the **Kettle River** are popular picks. Skiers and snowmobilers flock to the park during winter, but it's equally popular for hiking and biking during the summer.

▶▶ Banning State Park, www.dnr.state.mn.us

Nevada
Las Vegas to Death Valley National Park

Distance: 132 miles
Time: 2 hours, 42 minutes
Gas: $13.20
Route: US-95 North to NV-267

You may think of Las Vegas as a great jumping-off point for the Grand Canyon, but there are several other national parks accessible from the City of Sin. **Death Valley National Park** ($20.00 per vehicle) is just a few hours west of Las Vegas, where summer temperatures normally run around 120°F. But you can have fun despite the heat. Start off at **Badwater Basin**, the lowest point in North America, at 282 feet below sea level. Then stop by **Scotty's Castle** ($20.00 per vehicle for 7-day admission), an "engineer's dream home" built in the 1920s. Before you leave, check out **Dante's View,** a cliff that stands 5,000 feet above the desert floor, for wide-ranging views of Death Valley.

▶▶ Death Valley National Park, www.nps.gov/deva

> Tip: Go at night with a telescope for incredible star viewing.

Las Vegas to Zion National Park

About 160 miles east of Las Vegas is **Zion**, Utah's stunning first national park ($25.00 per vehicle). The **Kolob Arch**—one of the largest natural arches in the park—is located in the park's back-country and draws thousands of visitors each year. Hiking, biking, horseback riding, and camping options are plentiful, but if you'd rather stay in the car, try the **Zion Canyon Scenic Drive**, a 90-minute loop, for the best views.

▶▶ Zion National Park, www.nps.gov/zion

On the way . . . Bryce Canyon National Park

To complete your national park tour, drive another 85 miles north-east from Zion to Bryce Canyon. The landscape here is beyond spectacular, with white-tipped red rocks and tall spires of stone known as hoodoos. A 20-mile scenic drive takes you along the rim, where you can enjoy expansive views of the park against the sprawling backdrop of southern Utah, drive over a naturally formed arch bridge, and take a moment to enjoy **Bryce Point**, from which you can view the natural **Bryce Amphitheater.**

▶▶ Bryce Canyon National Park, www.nps.gov/brca

New York
New York to Long Island's North Fork Wine Country

> Distance: 84.3 miles
> Time: 1 hour, 47 minutes
> Gas: $8.43
> Route: I-495 East to Old Country Road/NY-58

Though well-heeled New Yorkers have been flocking to the Hamp-tons for decades, the North Fork is often overlooked as a destina-tion. But this is prime New York wine country (second only to the Finger Lakes region), with several dozen wineries and top-tier res-taurants. Year-round, thriving vineyards sprawl across the Fork, creating limitless opportunities for wine lovers. Grab a glass of bubbly at **Sparkling Pointe** winery's brand-new tasting room (open summer 2009), and taste some New American fare at the **North Fork Table and Inn** in Southold, which focuses on local, seasonal, and organic products, as well as special gatherings like winemaker's events and "slow-food" dinners.

▶▶ Long Island Wine Council, www.liwines.com

▶▶ Sparkling Pointe, www.sparklingpointe.com

▶▶ North Fork Table and Inn, www.northforktableandinn.com

On the way . . . Mattituck

Small town Mattituck is home to three well-known vineyards, all located within miles of each other. **Lieb Family Cellars** is an award-winning, family-run vineyard with free tastings and wine pairings with cheese and chocolate. One of the smallest, and best, tasting rooms in the area is **Sherwood House Vineyards** (tastings start at $7.00), another family-run operation, open since 1996, that is open to the public from Memorial Day through November. Try a grape stomp at Sherwood's annual **Harvest Celebration** in September, where there are plenty of wine, music, and merchandise discounts. In nearby Riverhead, you'll find **Martha Clara Vineyards** (tastings start at $5.00), another Fork wine haven. Take a wine break and check out Riverhead's **Hallockville Museum Farm** ($7.00 admission), 28 acres with more than 15 historic houses, barns, and outbuildings.

▶▶ Lieb Family Cellars, www.liebcellars.com

▶▶ Sherwood House Vineyards, www.sherwoodhousevineyards.com

▶▶ Martha Clara Vineyards, www.marthaclaravineyards.com

▶▶ Hallockville Museum Farm, www.hallockville.com

Cutchogue

Before this town was home to award-winning vineyards, Cutchogue was Native American territory. Explore that history at the nearby **Southold Indian Museum** ($2.00 suggested donation), which has the largest collection of Algonquin ceramic pottery in the world. For apple and pumpkin picking, a wagon ride, and a close-up look at a functioning beehive, stop by **Wickham's Fruit Farm** ($8.00 admission), one of the largest and oldest farms on the North Fork. Long Island's oldest winery is **Castello di Borghese,** where a $15.00 Winemaker's Walk tours you through the facilities and ends with a tasting. Learn how to make your own barrel of wine, from grape picking to bottling, at the members-only **Sannino's Bella Vita Vineyard Home Winemakers' Center,** and then bring home 275 bottles ($3,500 annual membership).

▶▶ Southold Indian Museum, www.southoldindianmuseum.org

▶▶ Wickham's Fruit Farm, www.wickhamsfruitfarm.com

▶▶ Castello di Borghese, www.castellodiborghese.com

▶▶ Sannino's Bella Vita Vineyard, www.sanninovineyard.com

Syracuse to Kingston, Ontario, Canada

Distance: 133 miles
Time: 2 hours, 15 minutes
Gas: $13.30
Route: I-81 North to Provincial Route 137 North to
Highway 401 North to Exit 617, Division Street

Kingston, Ontario, is the freshwater-diving capital of Canada. So what better way to get your feet wet than by exploring a few shipwrecks? Not your thing? Landlubbers can dive through piles of vintage clothing and sundry treasures at one of Kingston's many flea markets or head 25 miles north to **Frontenac Provincial Park** for hiking and biking in the summer and skiing and snowshoeing in the winter. History buffs with a hankering for 19th-century military life can plan an excursion to the UNESCO World Heritage site **Fort Henry,** where musical interludes by military bands and marching demonstrations by the Fort Henry Guard are usually on the agenda.

▶▶ Shipwreck sites, www.adventuredives.com/kingston.htm

▶▶ Flea markets, www.ontariofleamarkets.com

▶▶ Frontenac Provincial Park, www.frontenacpark.ca

▶▶ Fort Henry National Historic Site, www.forthenry.com

On the way . . . Wellesley Island
Just off I-81 in New York is Wellesley Island, which is composed of three major parks: The 2,600-plus-acre **Wellesley Island State Park** is best for swimming and boating; **Dewolf Point State Park** is popular among campers; and **Mary Island State Park,** accessible only by boat from the eastern tip of Wellesley Island, is ideal for hiking and enjoying views of the St. Lawrence River. Antiques aficionados can shop for anachronistic knickknacks at **Park Antiques.**

▶▶ New York State Parks, www.nysparks.state.ny.us

▶▶ Park Antiques, www.wellesleyisland.net/parkantiquesfront.htm

North Carolina
Raleigh to Mount Airy

Distance: 138 miles
Time: 2 hours, 21 minutes
Gas: $13.80
Route: I-40 West to US-421 North to US-52 North to Main Street

Mount Airy, hometown of Andy Griffith, is often compared with the fictitious Mayberry due to its small-town feel and picturesque landscape. A trip to the mountains practically guarantees some gentle breezes, and Mount Airy offers even more—an expansive countryside, vineyards, orchards, and storybook architecture. Take advantage of Andy Griffith's hometown's haunts and explore the **World's Largest Andy Griffith Collection** ($3.00 admission) and **Opie's Candy Store**. Exhausted by Griffith mania? Check out **Levering Orchard** in nearby Ararat, Virginia, for sweet and sour cherries, a variety of apples, peaches, nectarines, and pears. The area also plays host to three pick-your-own strawberry farms.

▶▶ World's Largest Andy Griffith Collection, www.visitmayberry.com

▶▶ Opie's Candy Store, www.opiescandystore.com

▶▶ Levering Orchard, www.leveringorchard.com

On the way . . . Yadkin Valley Wine Trail

At the base of the Blue Ridge Parkway is the Yadkin Valley, a 1.4-million-acre area that's home to some of the state's best wineries. **Old North State Winery and Brewery** offers tastings ($12.00), a social hour with wine and appetizers, and a dining experience with a range of satisfying dishes. Sample family reserve wines and limited releases at **Shelton Vineyards** ($20.00 admission) during the reserve tasting and tour.

▶▶ Old North State Winery and Brewery,
   www.oldnorthstatewinery.com

▶▶ Shelton Vineyards, www.sheltonvineyards.com

Siler City

Directly on the way to Mount Airy is the small community of Siler City, a historical town that's perfect for a lunchtime stop. **Horizon Cellars** ($4.00 tasting) is a boutique winery in Siler City, and the nearby **Southern Supreme Gourmet Specialties** gives tours and tastings of its nutty fruitcakes (signature item), jams, chocolates, cookies, and more.

▶▶ Horizon Cellars, www.horizoncellars.com

▶▶ Southern Supreme Gourmet Specialties, www.southernsupreme.com

Ohio
Cincinnati to Louisville, Kentucky

Distance: 98.5 miles
Time: 1 hour, 34 minutes
Gas: $9.85
Route: I-71 South to Exit 1A

See the bluegrass for yourself in Louisville. Even if there's no race happening at **Churchill Downs,** you can take a tour of the grounds and, from March 15 through November, have a "barn and backside" van tour of the stables and infield arranged by the **Kentucky Derby Museum** ($10.00 for adults). Then, check out another Louisville icon by touring the **Louisville Slugger Museum and Factory** ($10.00 admission). The giant baseball bat outside gives away its location, and best of all, this place will personalize a bat with your name! For a bit of history, the **Farmington Historic Plantation** ($9.00 admission) is a restored site that specializes in the culture that once dominated the South.

▶▶ Churchill Downs, www.churchilldowns.com

▶▶ Kentucky Derby Museum, www.derbymuseum.org

▶▶ Louisville Slugger Museum and Factory, www.sluggermuseum.org

▶▶ Farmington Historic Plantation, www.historichomes.org/farmington

On the way . . . Carollton

Get a glimpse of "real" rural Kentucky in Carrollton. Just off I-71 about halfway to Louisville, you can embark on a 2-hour country driving tour that takes you from **General Butler State Resort Park,** along the Ohio River, past the two-centuries-old **Masterson House,** and past picturesque farms, horse ranches, and barns. If you need a little more excitement, check out the **Kentucky Speedway** for year-round races, or take a tour of the areas that are off-limits during races, like the infield and a luxury suite, and even ride around the track in a van ($5.00).

▶▶ Carollton Tourism, www.carrolltontourism.com

▶▶ Kentucky Speedway, www.kentuckyspeedway.com

Pennsylvania
Philadelphia to Lancaster County

Distance: 69.4 miles
Time: 1 hour, 29 minutes
Gas: $6.94
Route: I-76 West to US-202 South to US-30 West

Lancaster County, a.k.a. Amish Country, is often referred to as the place that time forgot. This is where you'll find farms, factories, and families that operate as they have for centuries. The **Amish Experience** (starting at $8.95) will clue you in to the lay of the land and give you the history behind the area.

For incredible local produce, visit **Kitchen Kettle Village,** a 36-stand marketplace with fresh foods and handmade items. For a comprehensive list of markets, restaurants, and events, visit www.padutchcountry.com.

▶▶ Amish Experience, www.amishexperience.com

▶▶ Kitchen Kettle Village, www.kitchenkettle.com

> **Tip:** On a trip like this, dress modestly. Anything showy will likely be considered offensive, as is taking photographs without permission.

On the way . . . Adamstown

Just about 22 miles northeast of Amish Country is the self-proclaimed Antiques Capital of the USA. There's something for every taste here, from European antiques at the **Country French Collection,** to Victorian furniture at **Oley Valley Architectural Antiques,** and, if you don't know what you want, the **Adamstown Antique Gallery** in nearby Denver has 2,000 square feet filled with hundreds of dealers on-site, and even experts on hand to help you out.

▶▶ Adamstown antiques, www.antiquescapital.com

Pittsburgh to Erie

Distance: 128 miles
Time: 2 hours, 5 minutes
Gas: $12.80
Route: I-279 North to I-79 North

Directly north of Pittsburgh, this industrial city by the water probably has a lot more to offer than you imagined, especially when it comes to family-friendly activities. The **Erie Zoo** ($7.00 admission) and **Splash Lagoon Indoor Water Park Resort** (tickets start at $34.95) are two family favorites. Meanwhile, **Presque Isle State Park,** which has free admission, is a 3,200-acre National Natural Landmark with ample opportunities for hiking, biking, boating, and fishing along the Lake Erie coast. Or, if you prefer to stay in the car, just take PA-832 into the park and drive the 13-mile interior loop.

▶▶ Erie Zoo, www.eriezoo.org

▶▶ Splash Lagoon Indoor Waterpark, www.splashlagoon.com

▶▶ Presque Isle State Park, www.presqueisle.org

On the way . . . Allegheny National Forest

Take a slight detour east of Erie to the 512,000-acre **Allegheny National Forest** for a long walk along the Allegheny Reservoir. Campgrounds are plentiful here, but if you're staying for only a few hours, be sure to check out the waterfalls, such as **Hector Falls**, which you can see from an easy 1-mile hiking trail.

▶▶ Allegheny National Forest, www.fs.fed.us/r9/forests/allegheny

Tennessee
Nashville to Gatlinburg

Distance: 223 miles
Time: 3 hours, 45 minutes
Gas: $22.30
Route: I-40 East to TN-66

Though something of a tourist trap for its quaint, mountain-town goodness, there's no doubt that Gatlinburg has a prime location on the border of **Great Smoky Mountains National Park.** You'll quickly become familiar with the 8-mile loop along Glades and Buckhorn Roads and TN-321, home to eateries, art galleries, and shopping. Visit between early November and late February to catch **Gatlinburg Winter Magic,** when the city glitters with 3 million (energy-efficient) lights. And, while the Tennessee Aquarium in Chattanooga is well known in the state, locals prefer **Ripley's Aquarium of the Smokies** in Gatlinburg ($22.29 admission), which boasts more than 10,000 sea creatures.

▶▶ Great Smoky Mountains National Park, www.nps.gov/grsm

▶▶ Ripley's Aquarium of the Smokies,
www.ripleysaquariumofthesmokies.com

On the way . . . Chattanooga

Take a dip south into unassuming Chattanooga to ride on the steepest passenger railway in the world, which opened in 1895. The **Incline Railway** ($14.00 per ticket) has a 72.7 percent grade as it climbs Lookout Mountain, overlooking the entire city. Visit on a clear day and you'll catch sight of the Great Smoky Mountains, which are more than 100 miles away. The **Hunter Museum** of **American Art** ($8.00 admission), standing on a cliff over the Tennessee River, offers world-class exhibits from the 19th century and beyond. Traveling with your family? Try the **Creative Discovery Museum** ($8.95 admission), an interactive, hands-on, kid-friendly museum. And, while you may be miles from Memphis, don't miss out on authentic Memphis-style barbecue at one of the best spots in town, **Sticky Fingers**.

▶▶ Incline Railway, www.ridetheincline.com

▶▶ Hunter Museum of American Art, www.huntermuseum.org

▶▶ Creative Discovery Museum, www.cdmfun.org

▶▶ Sticky Fingers, www.stickyfingersonline.com

Texas
Houston to Austin

Distance: 185 miles
Time: 3 hours, 14 minutes
Gas: $18.50
Route: I-10 West to TX-80/US-183

Austin is an anomaly: a liberal college town awkwardly situated in a red state. But the good news is that Austin is packed with free concerts, comedy shows, and other events—just check the weekly *Austin Chronicle* for listings. Go to the **Capitol Visitors Center** for some local history and a free tour of this landmark, the country's largest state capitol building. The University of Texas at Austin's **Lady Bird Johnson Wildflower Center** ($7.00 admission) is a favorite for outdoor and butterfly lovers, who flock here to see the annual Monarch migration. The University of Texas also hosts a variety of tours that will acquaint you with the Austin area, like one of the 307-foot-tall **University of Texas Tower** ($5.00), which offers views of the campus and Austin from all directions. Beat the heat at Zilker Park's **Barton Springs Pool** ($3.00 admission), a natural aquifer that's a cool 68°F year-round.

▶▶ Capitol Visitors Center, www.tspb.state.tx.us/CVC/home/home.html

▶▶ Lady Bird Johnson Wildflower Center, www.wildflower.org

▶▶ University of Texas Tower, www.utexas.edu/tower

▶▶ Barton Springs Pool, www.ci.austin.tx.us/parks/bartonsprings.htm

On the way . . . Fredericksburg

Keep driving west from Austin to reach the little town of Fredericksburg, a spot that antiques lovers shouldn't miss. The **Fredericksburg Antique Mall,** made up of dozens of stores, is a favorite. But there's more to this place than just its antiques. How about its history? In the mid-1800s, Germans began settling in this southern city, making it a European center. The **Gillespie County Historical Society** houses one of its collections at the Vereins Kirche, or Society Church ($1.00 admission), which used to be both the town hall and the school in the 1800s, and the other at the **Pioneer Museum Complex** ($4.00 admission), which housed a general store and another schoolhouse. The **Texas Hill Country Wine Trail** takes you to 22 wineries in Texas, but wine enthusiasts should stop by the family-run **Fredericksburg Winery** (tastings start at $15.00), which has been around since 1978.

▶▶ Fredericksburg Antique Mall, 540-372-6894

▶▶ Gillespie County Historical Society, www.pioneermuseum.com

▶▶ Texas Hill Country Wine Trail, www.texaswinetrail.com

▶▶ Fredericksburg Winery, www.fbgwinery.com

Dallas to Tyler

Distance: 97.8 miles
Time: 1 hour, 41 minutes
Gas: $9.78
Route: I-30 East to US-80 East to I-20 East to Exit 556

Drive east of the big city to the small Texas town of Tyler. It's known as the Rose Capital of America, so don't miss the annual **Texas Rose Festival,** which takes place in October. At the very least, make sure you stop by the **Tyler Municipal Rose Garden,** the largest of its kind in the nation. If you prefer fauna to flora, catch a glimpse of wildlife at **Tyler State Park,** where you can rent a kayak or a mountain bike and explore the East Texas terrain at your own pace.

▶▶ Texas Rose Festival, www.texasrosefestival.com

▶▶ Tyler Municipal Rose Garden, www.texasrosefestival.com/museum/garden.htm

▶▶ Tyler State Park, www.tpwd.state.tx.us

On the way . . . Canton

Directly on the way to Tyler is the town of Canton, home to one of the largest flea markets in the world. You must bargain big at **First Monday Trade Days,** a flea market bazaar with all sorts of crafts and knickknacks (it actually begins on the Thursday before the first Monday of the month). Canton swells from approximately 3,000 people to nearly 100,000 during this monthly market's busiest season.

▶▶ First Monday Trade Days, www.firstmondaycanton.com

Utah
Salt Lake City to Ogden Valley

Distance: 53.7 miles
Time: 1 hour, 20 minutes
Gas: $5.37
Route: I-15 North to UT-79 to UT-39

One of the first things you'll notice about Ogden Valley is the monks—Trappist monks, that is. These Roman Catholic monks live in just 170 monasteries around the world, including the **Holy**

Trinity Abbey here, where you can purchase Trappist Creamed Honey (a crystallized honey spread) and other locally produced honeys, fine woodwork items, and rosaries. Nearby Huntsville may not have much, but be sure to stop by the **Shooting Star Saloon** for a bite of what keeps it in business: burgers. If you aren't worried about cholesterol, try the artery-clogging Star Burger, a double patty topped with knockwurst. Another huge draw comes every August, when enormous balloons are launched into the sky at the **Ogden Valley Balloon and Artist Festival.** And make sure you indulge in some of the food and crafts on the ground below.

▶▶ Holy Trinity Abbey, www.holytrinityabbey.com

▶▶ Shooting Star Saloon, 801-745-2002

▶▶ Ogden Valley Balloon and Artist Festival, www.ogdenvalleyballoonfestival.com

On the way . . . Park City

Take a quick detour east of Salt Lake City to **Park City Mountain Resort.** It's home to the world's first "green" roller coaster. The Alpine Coaster, which starts at $20.00 per ride, is completely silent and powered by gravity. You take a wind-powered ski lift up the mountain, get into a two-person *Jetsons*-esque car, then ride the rail down through the woods, controlling it with a hand brake, zipping through the trees and around banked turns. A bit farther south are the hot springs in Midway, including **Homestead Crater,** which is popular with swimmers, snorkelers, and scuba divers (don't be surprised to find divers here in the middle of winter).

▶▶ Park City Mountain Resort, www.parkcitymountain.com

▶▶ Homestead Crater, www.homesteadresort.com

Antelope Island State Park

What better way to experience the vast Great Salt Lake than to hang out in the middle of it? The 42-square-mile **Antelope Island State Park** ($9.00 per vehicle) is the largest of 10 islands in the lake, located just off I-15. Coyotes, elks, bobcats, and other animals share the space, but free-roaming American bison outnumber them all, with a herd of about 600.

> Tip: Visit in early November during the great bison roundup to watch cowboys corral each member of the herd for examination.

Hiking, biking, and cross-country skiing are three favorite activities, all well punctuated by a stop at **Buffalo Point Café and Bistro** for a scenic meal on the water.

▶▶ Antelope Island State Park, www.utah.com/stateparks/antelope_
island.htm

▶▶ Buffalo Point Café and Bistro, www.buffalopointinc.com

Washington
Seattle to Vancouver, British Columbia, Canada

Distance: 141 miles
Time: 2 hours, 25 minutes
Gas: $14.10
Route: I-5 North to Provincial Route 99 North to Exit 41B, Marine Drive West

Just keep driving north of Seattle and you'll reach Canada, eh? To get the flavor of local life, visit the **Granville Island Public Market** in the heart of one of Vancouver's liveliest communities. Every day, dozens of vendors open up shop to sell produce, baked goods, seafood, and desserts, as well as an eclectic mix of international specialties and cuisines—definitely try to stop by **Muffin Granny** to pick up a "scrumpet," a sconelike treat. And take a walk down **Railspur Alley**, where local artists set up shop along the street.

▶▶ Granville Island Public Market, www.granvilleisland.com/en/public_
market

On the way . . .

It's easy to travel from Vancouver to nearby islands, so on this trip, ditch the car and hop on **BC Ferries**.

▶▶ BC Ferries, www.bcferries.com

Victoria

It will cost you C$13.00 (about $10.00) to get to Victoria from Vancouver. Here, a heavy European influence is reflected in the architecture, but it maintains a small-town feel. The **Quw'utsun' Cultural and Conference Center** will give you the local history of the Cowichan Tribe. And, if you think mini toothpaste is cute, visit **Miniature World** (C$12.00, or about $10.00), which contains more than 85 scenes, including ornate dollhouses, the world's smallest sawmill, and one of the longest toy train railroads. See one of British Columbia's biggest attractions, the **Vancouver Aquarium** (C$20.00, or about $17.00), which houses more than 60,000 marine animals, including tropical reef sharks, dolphins, sea otters, and beluga whales.

▶▶ Quw'utsun' Cultural and Conference Center, www.quwutsun.ca

▶▶ Miniature World, www.miniatureworld.com

▶▶ Vancouver Aquarium, www.vanaqua.org

Washington, DC
Washington, DC, to Williamsburg, Virginia

Distance: 152 miles
Time: 2 hours, 35 minutes
Gas: $15.20
Route: I-395 South to I-95 South to I-295 South to I-64 East to Exit 238

"That the future may learn from the past," the slogan of Colonial Williamsburg, describes the essence of the city: a modern town living and loving our country's foundation. When you first get here, take the **Orientation Walk,** a 30-minute overview of the city featuring the latest updates on programs and dining options to help you focus your time in Williamsburg. At the Courthouse, experience a "live" court case that brings personal liberties and the rules of property into question. The guests (meaning you!) take on the roles of attorneys, justices, and defendants. When the sun sets, check out the **Original Ghosts of Williamsburg Candlelight Tour** ($10.00) and hear tales of colonial folklore and mystery that are left unexplained.

▸▸ Colonial Williamsburg, www.history.org

▸▸Original Ghosts of Williamsburg Candlelight Tour, www.theghosttour.com

Chesapeake Bay

The **Chesapeake Bay** is the largest estuary in the country, and the surrounding region includes a dozen states that are within reasonable driving distance. Visit the **Breezy Point Beach and Campground** for swimming locations and waterfront campgrounds. For some Maryland history, visit the **Maryland State House,** which dates back to 1772 and is the oldest capitol building still being used in the United States. The Continental Congress met in the famous Senate Chamber of the building to decide the future of our young country. And don't forget, the Maryland region of the Bay is a beautiful place to spend even just few hours.

▸▸ Chesapeake Bay, www.thechesapeakebay.com

▸▸ Breezy Point Beach and Campground, www.co.cal.md.us

▸▸ Maryland State House, www.msa.md.gov

▽ Additional Resources:

Road Trip America's Fuel Cost Calculator, www.roadtripamerica. com/fuel-cost-calculator.php

Gasoline Price Data for US Cities, www.fueleconomy.gov/feg/gasprices/states/index.shtml

CHAPTER 9

WHERE THE DOLLAR
IS KING

IN APRIL 2008, the euro was topping $1.60 and the cost of going to much of Europe was nothing short of prohibitive. The British pound was killing the dollar at the $2.00 level. At the end of the year, the euro dropped 20 percent, to $1.36. The Australian dollar cost just 67¢ against the US dollar, down from nearly $1.00 during the summer of 2008. Earlier in 2008, the Canadian dollar was worth more than the US dollar. And then it dropped to about 80¢. And the dollar is now becoming king in places like Korea, against that country's won. On December 15, 2008, Runzheimer International tracked some other currencies against the dollar and then estimated real travel costs for a meal, lodging, and car rental. For Americans, it's starting to look a whole lot better.

COUNTRY	LOCATION	CURRENCY (ABBREVIATION)	LUNCH PER DAY	LODGING PER DAY, INCLUDING TAX	CAR RENTAL PER DAY, INCLUDING TAX
Argentina	Buenos Aires	Peso (ARS)	56.54 (about $16.00)	528.29 (about $154.00)	260.71 (about $76.32)
Chile	Santiago	Peso (CLP)	9,562.70 (about $14.00)	90,592.00 (about $140.00)	25,363.80 (about $40.00)
India	Mumbai	Rupee (INR)	801.80 (about $17.00)	16,252.50 (about $344.00)	3,155.20 (about $66.00)
Jordan	Amman	Dinar (JOD)	17.14 (about $24.00)	93.94 (about $133.00)	98.48 (about $139.00)
Kenya	Nairobi	Shilling (KES)	978.04 (about $13.00)	8,327.00 (about $110.00)	5,223.30 (about $69.00)

COUNTRY	LOCATION	CURRENCY (ABBREVIATION)	LUNCH PER DAY	LODGING PER DAY, INCLUDING TAX	CAR RENTAL PER DAY, INCLUDING TAX
Mexico	Mexico City	Peso (MXN)	192.93 (about $15.00)	1,950.19 (about $150.00)	513.34 (about $40.00)
New Zealand	Auckland	Dollar (NZD)	24.12 (about $14.00)	224.00 (about $128.00)	97.60 (about $56.00)
Thailand	Bangkok	Baht (THB)	785.59 (about $23.00)	3,766.35 (about $109.00)	1,646.40 (about $48.00)
China	Shanghai	Yuan (CNY)	181.25 (about $26.00)	885.20 (about $130.00)	Not available
South Africa	Johannesburg	Rand (ZAR)	109.20 (about $11.00)	1,347.42 (about $140.00)	580.80 (about $60.00)

Wisconsin-based Runzheimer International is a management consulting firm that provides workforce mobility solutions relating to business vehicles, relocation, travel management, corporate aircraft, and virtual office programs. Lodging data provided to Runzheimer by Smith Travel Research. Average daily rates for hotels are for a first-class, centrally located hotel. Lunch is an average of representative entrées and beverages surveyed both in business hotel restaurants and in local restaurants.

The lesson here? You can travel like a king in Argentina, where the US dollar is worth more than three times the peso. The cab ride from the airport—about 21 miles—cost me about $5.00. I took five people out for dinner at the most expensive steak house in Buenos Aires—we're talking steaks, side dishes, wine. You name it, we ordered it. My tab? One hundred and four dollars.

In Mumbai, hotels that cater to Western tourists can be expensive, but you can find better value at Indian-owned three- or four-star properties that cater to business travelers. And when it comes to buying high-quality souvenirs, you'll find incredible deals there and in other cities like Bangkok.

Bottom line? An unexpected by-product of the global financial crisis is that the dollar got stronger. And as the dollar slowly begins inching its way back up the food chain, the deals are only going to get better and better. Travel is one of the largest industries in the world, employing the most people and being singularly responsible for the gross domestic products of more than 93 countries—and we now have increasing power to spend our travel dollars in countries that depend on it.

CHAPTER 10

TOURIST DISCOUNT CARDS

GO FOR THE DISCOUNTS, city by city.

A number of US and foreign cities—some doing a lot of promotion, but many others keeping it quiet—are offering discount cards. With a little advance planning, you can save a lot of money with these cards, as opposed to what you'd spend going à la carte on attractions, restaurants, transportation, and, in some cases, even hotels. While all of the prices and discounts listed below are for adults, most cards also reduce prices for children, so traveling families can save even more.

Go Orlando Card

Orlando, Florida

Available in 1-, 2-, 3-, 5-, or 7-day increments, this Orlando/ Kissimmee-area option gets you into 50 different attractions— except Disney World. If you're planning on spending significant time at Disney World, chances are you're not going to visit enough alternate attractions to make purchasing this card worthwhile. But if you've done Disney to death, the card does cover Kennedy Space Center, Daytona 500 Experience, Gatorland, and the Orlando Museum of Art, to name a few. It also covers some family-friendly activities in Miami, like the zoo, museums, and various city tours. But the bottom line is that you'll have to cram in the activities to make this pricey card worthwhile.

3-Day Card: $159.99

Without card:
Gatorland: $22.99
Daytona 500 Experience: $25.56
Boggy Creek Airboat Ride: $24.56
Congo River Adventure Golf: $10.95
Haunted Grimm House: $10.00
Ripley's Believe It or Not! Orlando Odditorium: $18.95
WonderWorks House of Oddities: $20.00
Miami 1-day tour from Orlando (including transportation):
    $69.00
Total: $202.01
Savings: $42.02

▶▶ www.goorlandocard.com

Go Los Angeles Card
Los Angeles, California

Available in 1-, 2-, 3-, 5-, and 7-day increments, the value of a Los Angeles card really depends on how much driving you're willing to do. Free activities on Hollywood Boulevard are miles from the *Queen Mary* in Long Beach, which you'll also board for free. So, you'll have to plan well and pack in a few activities each day to make it worthwhile. For example, you can tour the Hollywood Wax Museum and Guinness World Records Museum and then spend your afternoon and evening at Universal Studios Hollywood. The next day, visit the *Queen Mary* and take a Spirit cruise in Long Beach. On your 3rd day, go to Six Flags Magic Mountain.

3-Day Card: $159.99

Without card:
Hollywood Wax Museum/Guinness World Records Museum
    combo: $17.95

Hollywood Museum: $15.00
Universal Studios Hollywood: $67.00
Queen Mary: $24.95
Aquarium of the Pacific: $20.95
Spirit Cruises Super Circle or Coastal Cruise: $18.00
Six Flags Magic Mountain: $59.99
Total: $223.84
Savings: $63.85

▶▶ www.golosangelescard.com

Go San Diego Card

San Diego, California

Once Knott's Berry Farm was added to the list of attractions discounted with the Go San Diego Card, its value shot way up. Before that, the 2-day card for $89.99 and the 3-day for $119.99 only made the cut for travelers going to the San Diego Zoo, LEGOLAND California, and perhaps a harbor tour or a museum. You still have to pack in a good amount of pretty exhausting activities to get your money's worth, but at least they're top-tier attractions.

3-Day Card: $119.99

Without card:
San Diego Zoo: $35.00
LEGOLAND California: $62.00
Knott's Berry Farm: $44.99
Harbor Cruise (Full Bay Tour): $25.00
USS *Midway* Museum: $17.00
Total: $183.99
Savings: $64.00

▶▶ www.gosandiegocard.com

New York CityPass

New York, New York

The New York CityPass is valid for 9 days from the first use. It includes admission to five museums: the Empire State Building Observatory, the Museum of Modern Art, the Metropolitan Museum of Art and the Cloisters, the Guggenheim, and the American Museum of Natural History and Hayden Planetarium. Plus you get your choice of a Circle Line sight-seeing cruise or admission to the Statue of Liberty and Ellis Island. The CityPass also includes various other discounts, such as $5 off a hop-on, hop-off bus tour of the city and 15 percent off at Bloomingdale's with a purchase of $100 or more.

If you're a real museum buff, this is the deal for you. It's generally not a good idea to cram in more than one museum a day—especially considering the size of these venues—but the 9-day span of this pass actually makes it feasible to hit them all.

> Tip: Another little-known discount unrelated to the CityPass: Non-New Yorkers get 11 percent off all purchases at Bloomingdale's and Macy's. Best of all, that discount is on top of regular sale and clearance discounts. Note that it is not valid for items like furniture, cosmetics, and electronics. Just show your out-of-state driver's license at the customer service department and you'll get a coupon for 11 percent off.

If you're comfortable navigating the city and plan to shun taxis, go for an MTA MetroCard. The 1-day Fun Pass costs only $7.50 for unlimited subway and local bus rides from first use until 3:00 a.m. the following day.

New York CityPass: $74.00

Without card:

Empire State Building Observatory: $18.45

American Museum of Natural History and Hayden
    Planetarium Space Show: $24.00

Guggenheim: $18.00
Museum of Modern Art: $20.00
Metropolitan Museum of Art and the Cloisters: $20.00
Circle Line Sightseeing Cruise: $27.00
Total: $127.45
Savings: $53.45

▶▶ www.citypass.com/city/ny.html

> Tip: Don't forget that passes may improve your experience even when they
> don't save you a lot of money. If a pass lets you skip admission lines at a
> museum or theme park, especially in the high season, you'll save a lot of
> time and headaches. Similarly, a transportation pass means you don't have
> to worry about fishing around for bus fare.

SydneyPass

Sydney, Australia

This is only a 3-, 5-, or 7-day transportation pass, but the benefit is that it permits use of both sight-seeing and public transportation services, plus two trips on Airport Link. Chances are that you won't save more than few dollars, but it does save you the hassle of having to purchase a ticket every time you travel within Sydney. The value also goes up the farther you travel in the city, because fares vary by distance.

If you're planning to use primarily public transportation, opt for the DayTripper pass, which gives you access to the CityRail train, Sydney buses, and Sydney ferries, plus some discounts to attractions, for AU$16.00 (about $10.72).

3-Day Pass: AU$110.00 (about $72.00)

Without card:

Airport Link (international terminal to Circular Quay, round-trip): AU$22.60

Sydney Explorer: AU$39.00

Bondi Explorer: AU$39.00
Sydney Ferries (round-trip): AU$5.20
CityRail: AU$10.00 (estimate)
Total: AU$115.80
Savings: AU$5.80 (about $3.80)

▶▶ www.sydneybuses.info/tourist-services/sydneypass.htm

Paris Museum Pass

Paris, France

As the name might suggest, this pass was made for museum buffs—not for people who think they'll *turn into* museum buffs once they arrive in Paris. Be realistic about how many museums you're really going to visit in one trip. The 2-day pass for €30.00 (about $40) isn't going to save anyone money because many of the major museums charge between €6.00 and €10.00 (about $8.00 and $13.00) for admission. But the 6-day pass at €60.00 (about $76.00) can be a good deal. And these passes aren't just for the Louvre; you get entrance to more than 60 museums and monuments in and around Paris, plus you get to skip the lines, which in peak seasons can be highly worthwhile.

2-Day Pass: €30.00 (about $40.00)

Without card:
Musée du Louvre: €9.00
Musée d'Orsay: €9.00
Tours de Notre-Dame: €7.50
Arc de Triomphe: €9.00
Musée de la Publicité: €8.00
Musée Rodin: €6.00
Total: €48.50
Savings: €18.50 (about $24.30)

▶▶ www.parismuseumpass.com/en/home.php

I Amsterdam Card

Amsterdam, the Netherlands

Available in 1-, 2-, and 3-day versions, this card includes free, unlimited access to public transportation (but not trains or airport transfers) and free or discounted admission to 30 attractions, plus restaurant discounts. At €33.00 (about $42.00), the 1-day pass is unlikely to be worthwhile. But if you cram in a lot of museum-going, the value of the 3-day pass goes up.

3-Day Pass: €53.00 (about $66.00)

Without card:
Transportation: at least €19.20 (three rides at €6.40 per ride)
Anne Frank House: €8.00
Van Gogh Museum: €12.50
Amsterdam Historic Museum: €10.00
Hortus Botanicus (botanic garden): €7.00
Jewish Historical Museum: €7.50
Total: €64.20
Savings: €11.20 (just under $15.00)

▶▶ www.iamsterdamcard.com

Prague Card

Prague, Czech Republic

This card offers free access to more than 50 museums and galleries, Prague Castle, Old Town, and more. Public transportation isn't included, but can be added on at a rate of CZK 330 (about $15.50) for 3 days. Odds are that this pass won't be worth your while, considering the low entry fees at many of the included sites.

4-day pass: CZK 790 (about $39.00)

Without card:
Prague Castle: CZK 150
Powder Tower: CZK 50

Malá Strana Bridge Towers: CZK 50
Czech Literature Museum: CZK 30
Vyšehrad Gallery: CZK 10
Trade Fair Palace: CZK 300
Total: CZK 590
Savings: You lose CZK 200 (about $10)

▶▶ www.praguecard.biz

VENICECard

Venice, Italy

Available in 3- and 7-day passes, this card includes airport bus transfer (you can add on a boat transfer for another €23.00), public transportation (collectively known as Actv for bus and *vaporetto* services), admission to 12 museums and 16 churches, and—most importantly—two toilet entrances a day. There are two price levels based on age: tourists 29 years and younger are considered "juniors," while those 30 and over are "seniors."

3-Day Senior Card: €71.90 (about $90.00)

Without card:
Alilaguna airport transport (one-way): €25.00
Vaporetto (water bus): at least €19.50 (€6.50 for 1 hour of
     travel on each of 3 days)
Museo Correr: €15.50
Venice Museo Archeologico: €12.00
Chiesa di Santa Maria Formosa: €3.00
Jewish Museum: €3.00
Two toilet entrances a day (€1.00 each on each of 3 days): €6.00
Total: €84.00
Savings: €12.10 (about $15.75)

The Museum Pass, which costs €18.00 ($22.73) and is good for 3 months, is something you may as well keep in your back pocket. It covers one admission to all of the civic museums, including the Doge's Palace and Museo Correr, and is worth it even if you only visit two sites.

However, if museums aren't on your itinerary, a better bet is the stripped-down transport-only card. A 3-day pass, including airport boat transfer, is €60.50 (about $78.00). Getting around Venice is easiest by foot and by *vaporetto,* which, at €6.50 ($8.20) per hour of travel time, quickly adds up. But what makes this card really worthwhile is that it includes a ride on the Alilaguna airport water bus, a €25.00 ($32.00) value, which is quite an experience (but take it only one way and then take the more economical bus back to the airport).

▶▶ www.hellovenezia.it/jsp/en/venicecard/index.jsp

Barcelona City Card
Barcelona, Spain

A 3-day pass gets you unlimited transportation on public subways, buses, trams, and trains and 20 percent off the airport bus. You won't get free entry to any museum on your list, but you can save between 20 and 50 percent on must-see sites like the Picasso Museum. Unless you cram in a lot of traveling and museum-hopping during those 3 days, you're not likely to save much, but you can avoid paying a fare each time you travel.

The Barcelona Bus Turistic, the local sight-seeing bus, is not included, but a pass for it can be purchased as a separate package for 1 day (€20, or $25) or 2 days (€26, or $33), and also comes with its own discounts on sights and attractions.

And if you think you'll visit more than two or three museums, opt for the articketBCN, which offers one free admission to seven major museums for €20.00 (about $25.00) and can be used for 6 months from the start date. The facilities included are the

Museu Picasso, Centre de Cultura Contemporània de Barcelona, Fundació Antoni Tàpies, La Pedrera de Caixa Catalunya, Fundació Joan Miró, Museu d'Art Contemporani de Barcelona, and Museu Nacional d'Art de Catalunya.

▶▶ Barcelona Bus Turistic: www.tmb.net/en_US/turistes/busturistic/bitllets.jsp

▶▶ articketBCN: www.articketbcn.org/en

3-Day Pass: €30 (about $38)

Without card:
Transportation: at least €3.90 (three rides at €1.30 per ride)
Museu Frederic Marès: €4.20
Museu Picasso (half off): €4.50
Museu de Ceràmica: €4.20
Total: €16.80
Savings: You lose €13.20 (about $17.20)

▶▶ www.barcelona-tourist-guide.com/en/general/barcelona-card.html

Budapest Card

Budapest, Hungary

Two- and 3-day passes offer unlimited travel on public transit, free access to permanent museum exhibitions and discounts to temporary exhibitions, half-price sight-seeing buses, and discounts at public bathhouses and restaurants. However, some of the museums included are already free. Also, because Hungary has yet to adopt the euro, the favorable exchange rate means that you won't spend more than a few dollars on public transportation or entry fees anyway. But because you're likely to take the subway, bus, trolley, or tram to get around the city, the card will save you the headache of paying per ride and also expose you to sites you might not have known about otherwise.

3-Day Pass: HUF 8,000 (about $38.00)

Without card:

Single transportation ticket: at least HUF 690 (three rides at HUF 230 per ride)

Budapest History Museum: HUF 1,100

Memento Park–Statue Park: HUF 1,500

Museum of Fine Arts: HUF 3,200

Sightseeing bus (half off): HUF 3,250

Total: HUF 9,740

Savings: HUF 1,740 (about $8.60)

▶▶ www.budapestinfo.hu/en/budapest_card

Bangkok Discounts

Bangkok, Thailand

There is no discount card for Bangkok, but several shopping outlets offer a 5 percent discount if you flash your passport. This includes stores in the Siam Paragon, the Emporium, Robinsons Department Store, and the MBK Center. There's nothing wrong with that as long as you're comfortable with holding on to your passport while you're out and about.

▶▶ www.bangkok.com/shopping-vat-refund

Oyster Card

London, England

This prepaid transportation pass can store up to £90 (about $135.00) and can be used on the London Tube, bus, trams, DLR (light rail), London Overground, and even select National Rail services. It caps the amount you're charged on each mode of transport to ensure that you get the lowest fee. For example, London buses and trams cost £2 ($3.00) per ride, but with an Oyster card, you'll pay £1 (about $1.50). For the Tube, DLR, and

Overground, the maximum price to travel in touristy Zones 1 and 2 is £6.70 ($9.80) during peak times and £5.10 (about $7.50) off-peak. Bottom line here? Plan ahead so you don't load up the card with too much money and you'll save.

▶▶ www.tfl.gov.uk/tickets/oysteronline/2732.aspx

Entertainment Books

You may have come across an entertainment book at a local store or from a high school student trying to raise money. These books are jam-packed with coupons and discounts that add up to a lot more than you pay for them, which is usually $25 to $40. That is, of course, if you use them!

No doubt about it, entertainment books can be impressive-looking packages. The New York City book, for example, has 380 pages and an estimated $16,400 in savings and discounts at 189 dining establishments, 134 attractions, and 220 stores.

Some of the travel savings in the book are significant, or at least unique. The entertainment books' publisher partners with certain travel providers to offer, for example, 5 percent off any American Airlines flight for up to six people, which is a rarity for any airline these days. (Of course, the catch is that you can only use it one time, and the likelihood of buying six tickets at once is pretty low.)

You can also save on car rentals from Budget, Enterprise, Hertz, and National. The good news is that the deals extend for a year and a half, so you're not stuck with a bunch of worthless coupons if you don't use them right away. Bargains include free upgrades, $20 off weekend rentals, and 20 percent plus $20 off weekly rentals.

Hotel deals are also ubiquitous, but they involve rebates from nationwide chains, not local hotels. One important caution here: In many cases, the percentage discounts offered for hotel rooms are essentially discounts against a hotel's highest rate. By comparison, you may be eligible for a meaningful discount on a hotel room with a card you're already carrying, such as an AARP or AAA card.

A major problem is that these books aren't well organized geographically, so as a traveler, you may not have the know-how to maximize your usage for a particular city. The New York City book, for example, covers Manhattan, Brooklyn, Queens, the Bronx, and Staten Island, but the coupons are all jumbled together. So if you happen to be eating at a pizza place that's listed in the index, you're in luck. On the other hand, it's a good way to try a local restaurant that you may not have heard of otherwise. But chances are that on a 3-day trip to New York, you won't have much opportunity to use many of the discounts aside from those for the major tourist attractions.

Some of the chain-store discounts these books offer are universal, so geography won't get in your way when using them. Most books offer pages of $6.50 movie tickets at any AMC theater, for example. But in the Orlando book, a coupon for a free sundae at Carvel isn't tied to any particular store, while one for Baskin-Robbins is. In the same book, a free Big Mac is available from any participating McDonald's in several counties.

CHAPTER 11

FREE ACTIVITIES

EVEN IN THE WORST ECONOMIC TIMES, you can still find valuable experiences, and sometimes transportation, for free. As recently as a year ago, the financial equation of travel was unbalanced—in many cases, it was inexpensive to get to a destination, but very expensive to be at that destination. And that tradeoff wasn't pleasant. That bad situation was compounded by the weakness of the US dollar against so many foreign currencies. But now, regardless of unfavorable exchange rates, with a little advance planning, you can save some serious money on the ground even in some of the world's most expensive cities. And believe it or not, there's a method to the madness.

Freebies on Wheels

A free bike ride around a new city? A strange concept, but it's one that's taking off in Europe and maybe even in your own backyard.

> Tip: Audio tours are an easy way to hear some local history while you bike or walk around without a tour guide. And these days, it's easy to download specialty audio tours on your iPod or MP3 player. Chicago Tourism (www.downloadchicagotours.com) offers free downloadable tours with themes like the history of Chicago blues music and a kid-centric tour of the city. Boston also has free audio tours of the Fort Point Channel and the downtown harbor area available at www.bostonharborwalk.com/audio_tour. And Tourcaster.com (www.tourcaster.com) is an aggregate site offering low-cost (about $10) downloads of audio tours for walking and driving in cities worldwide.

Tip: Ready to take a hike? You can find hiking trails near major urban centers at www.localhikes.com, but also check with state trail associations to see what they say are the best spots.

Perhaps the best-known self-service bike rental program is in **Paris, France.** *Vélib'* was launched in 2007 and there are now at least 20,000 bikes available at 1,450 stations throughout the city. The way it works is that users, who must be age 14 or older, sign up for a subscription that allows an unlimited number of rentals in a particular time period—a day (€1.00, or about $1.26), a week (€5.00, or about $6.29), or a year (€29.00, or about $36.50). You just swipe your card, choose your bike from an on-screen menu, and take off! The first half hour is free, which, in theory, means you can ride around for 30 minutes, swap bikes at another stand, and continue going—for free! If you keep a bike for longer than 30 minutes, your card is charged incrementally: €1.00 for the first half hour, €2.00 (about $2.50) for the second additional half hour, and €4.00 (about $5.30) for every half hour thereafter. If you don't return the bike by the end of your subscription, you will be charged €150.00 (just under $190.00).

▶▶ www.en.velib.paris.fr

But Paris wasn't the first French city to offer this service. It was actually inspired by a similar program in **Lyon** known

Los Angeles: What better way to enjoy Tinseltown than to watch a TV-show taping? These live tapings are free; you just have to book them in advance. Check out resources like Audiences Unlimited and TVTix.com to sign up to be in the audience of your favorite show.

▶▶ www.tvtickets.com

▶▶ www.tvtix.com

as *vélo'v*, which was launched 2 years earlier. Locals tend to use their existing transportation passes, but visitors can purchase a *vélo'v* card for €1.00 and use it for up to 7 days. Rentals here are free for the first 30 minutes, €1.00 for 30 to 90 minutes, and €2.00 for each hour thereafter, for up to 24 hours per rental.

▸▸ www.velov.grandlyon.com

In **Switzerland,** both **Zürich** and **Bern** offer self-service bike rentals between May and October (except for one location in Zürich that offers it year-round). The *Züri rollt* (Zürich Rolls) program features more than 200 bikes (as well as skateboards and scooters) available at five stops throughout the city: Globus City shopping center, Oerlikon–Swissôtel hotel, the Opera House, the Enge train station, and the main Zürich railway station. You just drop off a CHF 20 (about $17.00) deposit and an ID card at one of the locations, and you can take off with a free bicycle between 8:00 a.m. and 9:30 p.m. (You have to return the bike to the same location.) Similar programs also exist in Geneva, Neuchâtel, and several other Swiss cities.

▸▸ www.zuerirollt.ch and www.bernrollt.ch (in Swiss German)

In a city as expensive as **Copenhagen, Denmark,** travelers will be grateful for any freebies. The *Bycyklen København* program runs between April and November and features 110 stations with 2,000 bikes. Insert a deposit of DKK 20 (about $3.38) into an

Denver: With the economy crashing around us, go straight to the source with a visit to the United States Mint. Tours are free and cover the craftsmanship and designs of US coins from past to present.

▶▶ www.usmint.gov/mint_tours

automated machine and pick your bike. One word of warning: You have to stay within the city bike zone, which encompasses most of central Copenhagen. If you stray beyond the borders, you may face a hefty fine. (Don't worry—you get a map with the bike.) The program works on the honor system, and there is no limit on how long you can keep the bike. Chances are, though, that you won't be packing these red and blue beauties in your suitcase.

▶▶ www.bycyklen.dk

Keep your eyes peeled for bright, lime green bikes around **Helsinki, Finland.** These are the official bikes of the Citybike program, launched in 2000. As in Copenhagen, you just pay a €2.00 deposit and take off for an unlimited time. You get the deposit back when you return the bike to any of the 26 stands around the city center. And remember to stay within the city center limits, which is a designated bike zone.

▶▶ www.hel.fi

Seattle: Though you'd think Seattlelites get wet enough in the winter, you'll find a number of free wading pools and "spray parks" scattered throughout the city during the summertime. These are actually city-run projects designed to keep locals and visitors cool while conserving water.

▶▶ www.seattle.gov/PARKS/wadingpools.asp

Atlanta: Remember that our National Park System doesn't just include parks. It also includes historic sites, memorials, and other areas with educational value. The Martin Luther King Jr. National Historic Site is a local gem that covers a stretch of Auburn Avenue in the Sweet Auburn district. You can take free, self-guided tours of sites like the Historic Ebenezer Baptist Church, where King and his father preached; the moving King Center memorial; and more. You can also join a free guided tour of King's birthplace.

▶▶ www.nps.gov/malu

Oslo, Norway's *Bysykkel* (City Bikes) program has more than 1,200 bikes and charges visitors 70 kroner (about $10.00) a day. The maximum rental time is 3 hours, but, of course, you can simply return your bike and rent another one at no additional fee. You can rent between the hours of 6:00 a.m. and midnight, but you can return the bike at any time of the day to one of the 90 or so stations around the city. Similar programs are available in **Drammen** and **Trondheim, Norway.**

▶▶ www.oslobysykkel.no and http://www.adshel.no/index2.html (in Norwegian)

In **Brussels, Belgium,** the Cyclocity program costs visitors €1.50 (about $2.00) a week or €10.00 (about $12.50) a year. The short-term card, geared toward visitors, gets you a bike for €0.50 (about 70¢) for the first 30 minutes and €1.00 for every hour after that. Note that Brussels has only about 250 bikes for the whole city.

▶▶ www.cyclocity.be

In **Vienna, Austria,** the Citybike Wein tourist card is available for €2.00 a day and allows you to rent at any of the 58 stations scattered throughout the city. First, you have to register online for a one-time fee of €1.00. The first hour of bike rental is free, the second is €1.00, the third costs €2.00, and then it's €4.00 (about $5.00) for the fourth and every hour thereafter, up to 120 hours. After that, you'll be charged a flat rate of €600.00 (just over $754.00), which means you'll have just bought a very expensive souvenir that you won't even be able to fit into your carry-on.

▶▶ www.citybikewien.at

In **Barcelona, Spain,** things are a bit trickier. The program, named Bicing, requires that you sign up with a credit card at a site that's only in Catalan and Spanish. Your registration is mailed in about 5 days, so put in your hotel's address and alert the front desk ahead of time that it will be arriving. You won't have a problem spotting the bikes around the city—they're red and white and adorned with the Bicing logo. The yearly subscription is €24.00 (about $30.00); the first half hour is free and each additional half hour costs €0.30 (about 37¢) for up to 2 hours. The bike program operates 24 hours a day on Fridays and Saturdays, but shuts down between midnight and 5:00 a.m. Sundays through Thursdays.

▶▶ www.bicing.com (in Catalan and Spanish)

Seville, Spain, currently has 2,500 bikes available at 250 stations throughout the city. You can pay €5.00 (about $6.30) per week or €10.00 a year, then get the first 30 minutes free. With the long-term deal, you pay €0.50 for the first hour after the initial free period, and €1.00 for every hour thereafter. The short-term rates are double that.

▶▶ http://en.sevici.es

New York City: Want the best view of the Statue of Liberty without the crowds? Skip the ferry to Ellis Island and instead hop on the Staten Island Ferry. The 25-minute ride is absolutely free.

▶▶ www.siferry.com

The concept of renting a bicycle has grown so popular that we're trying it out right here at home. In the summer of 2008, **Washington, DC,** launched its SmartBike DC program. A $40.00 annual subscription gets you a smart card that activates a bike at any of the 10 stations around the city. Like many of the European bike programs, this one is funded by Clear Channel Outdoor, which makes its money from outdoor advertisements. So, if this program takes off, you may soon be seeing it in other cities around the United States.

▶▶ www.smartbikedc.com

Free Walking Tours

I'm not a big fan of bus tours, but I do believe in getting up close and personal with a walking tour of a new city. Not only do you get to explore off-the-beaten-path areas (without getting hopelessly lost), but guides—often local historians—will also share colorful stories and details. And best of all, many of these tours are free!

One of the most popular programs in the country is **San Francisco's** City Guides, founded in 1978, which offers up to 45 different walking tours year-round. Volunteers lead 1½- and 2-hour tours with themes such as the 1906 earthquake, local ghost stories, and the first mural Diego Rivera painted in the United States, which includes an up-close look at it, even though it's normally closed to the public.

▶▶ San Francisco City Guides, 415-557-4266, www.sfcityguides.org

New York City has so many free and low-cost walking tours that your best bet is to check out the *Village Voice,* the local weekly alternative paper, or Web sites like NewYorkology, which is a gold mine of information on how to do New York on the cheap. You can find everything from a tour of an abandoned railway tunnel under Atlantic Avenue in Brooklyn, to a tour of famous movie and TV sites, to a walking tour of Hasidic neighborhoods.

Big Apple Greeters, perhaps the best known of the bunch, is based on the principle of showing out-of-towners that New York isn't a hostile and expensive big city. You fill out an online form at

Miami: The historic Biltmore Hotel offers three free tours every Sunday when you can hear anecdotes about the hotel's famous guests, from mob shootouts to ghostly hauntings.

▶▶ biltmorehotel.com

least 4 weeks before arriving, but to do so, you must have a confirmed hotel reservation (or, if you're staying with a friend, a local home phone number with an answering machine or voice mail); tours are limited to one to six people traveling together. Once you arrive, your volunteer greeter meets you at your hotel for a 2- to 4-hour walk through specific neighborhoods (your choice or theirs, a decision you make when filling out the online form). There's no cost involved (even tipping is banned), but there's also no guarantee that you'll get a tour—they get at least 1,000 requests a month and have 300 greeters. This model has been so successful that Greeter Network now offers similar programs in cities like Houston, Chicago, Fairbanks, Paris, and Toronto, all of which are accessible through the Big Apple Greeters Web site.

▶▶ www.newyorkology.com www.bigapplegreeter.org

In our nation's capital, **DC By Foot** is an hour-and-15-minute tour starting at the Washington Monument and ending at the Lincoln Memorial. It's not a complicated walk, but the enthusiastic guides make it fun for younger travelers—and adults who need a flashback to their junior high field trip.

▶▶ www.dcbyfoot.com

In **several European cities,** a lesser-known program called Like-a-Local offers experiences led by, you guessed it, local guides. Choose from three categories—Live, Go, and Eat—and you'll find everything from a Belgian cottage available for rent, a tour of Antwerp's diamond sector, to a tapas crawl with a Barcelonan foodie. Like-a-Local also operates in major cities like Paris, New York, and Rome, but for now those listings are limited.

▶▶ www.like-a-local.com

Austin: For a walk on the quirkier side, take a look at the Cathedral of Junk. Longtime Austin resident Vince Hannemann has spent more than 2 decades creating the soaring, cathedral-like sculpture in his backyard, made out of more than 60 tons of junk—everything from broken bicycles to old road signs to glass bottles. Inside, there are rooms, stairways, and even a "Throne Room" with a throne made out of, well, junk. Free tours are by appointment only.

▶▶ 512-299-7413

And now, free walking tours are becoming all the rage in . . . **Japan?** A **Tokyo** walking tour launched in the summer of 2008 takes place every Saturday from 1:00 p.m. to 3:00 p.m. The idea is to have local guides practice their English while giving you a personal tour from Tokyo Station to the East Garden of the Imperial Palace, with many points in between. Volunteer guides get around any language barriers by reading from a Japanese history book translated into English. Just head to the Marunouchi Central Entrance at Tokyo Station and look for someone carrying a Free Walking Tour sign.

▶▶ www.freewalkingtour.org

Las Vegas: Vegas is all about spectacle, including freebies like Bellagio's dancing fountains, the battle of the gods at Caesars Palace, and the volcano in front of the Mirage. But if you want to get off the Strip, head to Fremont Street's pedestrian zone for a nightly sound and light show that soars 90 feet high. Also check out the Neon Museum, which showcases signs from casinos of days gone by.

▶▶ www.vegasexperience.com

CHAPTER 12

DINING ON A BUDGET

YOU'D THINK THAT with an economic crisis and a continuing financial meltdown, many fine-dining restaurants would be empty. Think again. During the last 3 months of 2008, expensive restaurants in cities all across America were packed. Could it be that we're a country in denial?

I'm convinced it was something else: that mass "last supper" mentality. People were saying, "I have no idea if I'll be employed in 2009," or "I may not even have a credit card in 2009, so . . . ka-*ching!*"

Well, you still have to eat. And some of us would like to think you can still eat well in a very bad economy without refinancing your mortgage, which probably has already been refinanced anyway. Can you go out for a nice lunch for under $50.00 for two? Have an elegant dinner for less than $100.00 for two? How about much less than that?

Yes, you can do it. And under no circumstance am I recommending that you lock yourself inside some fast-food prison. With a little advance planning, you can eat healthfully and within a constricted budget. You may not be living high in hard times, but you can dine in style.

A huge opportunity to do this is to take advantage of a city during its Restaurant Week, when restaurants ranging from midprice to top-tier open their doors (and menus) for a fixed price. Meals are typically three-course prix fixe (appetizer, entrée, and dessert) with at least two options per course from the restaurant's regular menu. The drawbacks? Don't expect to see overly pricey or signature items on the menu, and the predetermined price doesn't include beverages, tax, or tip.

That said, perhaps the best part about Restaurant Week, besides the food, is that it generally takes place during a city's low seasons to draw in visitors—think late winter to early spring, and late summer to early fall, which is also when you're going to find savings on airfare and accommodations. And if you're a local, this is your chance to try out a five-star restaurant for a fraction of the price. (Note that all dates below are for 2009 only.)

> **Tip:** Many participating restaurants allow diners to make reservations online at www.opentable.com. Don't get shut out at the door—book your table at least a week in advance.

San Diego, California

Dates: January 11–16; September 13–18
Prices: $20.00, $30.00, or $40.00 for a three-course dinner
Here's a new twist on a dining concept: San Diego's Restaurant Week has partnered with Girl Scouts of the USA, so this year, the city's top chefs will create menu items using those delicious Thin Mints, Samoas, and Tagalongs. Now in its 5th year, this San Diego event features more than 150 restaurants. You can choose how many dining dollars you want to spend, with restaurants offering $20.00, $30.00, or $40.00 menus.

▶▶ www.sandiegorestaurantweek.com

San Francisco, California

Dates: January 15–31; June 1–15
Prices: $21.95 for a three-course lunch; $34.95 for a three-course dinner

More than 100 restaurants participate in San Francisco's Dine About Town, now entering its 8th year. Some of the top-tier establishments include Roy's restaurant, where a single sushi roll will normally cost you between $11.00 and $18.00, and One Market, where a regularly priced dinner entrée starts at $20.00.

▶▶ www.onlyinsanfrancisco.com/dineabouttown

New York, New York

Dates: January 18–23 and 25–30; early summer
Prices: $24.07 for a three-course lunch; $35.00 for a three-course dinner

No doubt about it, this is the time to dine at legendary New York restaurants like Blue Water Grill, Nobu, and Aquavit without breaking the bank. Now entering its 18th year, New York's Restaurant Week has become the model that several other cities use to bring in business during the slower tourist season. Just how affordable are we talking? Well, a lunch appetizer at Blue Water Grill normally costs between $8.00 and $13.00, while a tempura dinner at Nobu is priced at $28.00. There are also participating restaurants in Queens and Brooklyn, so think of this as an opportunity to go off the beaten path. Note that New York Restaurant Week prices are good only from Sunday through Friday.

▶▶ www.nycgo.com/restaurantweek

Tip: When visiting a new city, head straight to the farmers' market to experience fresh, local, and affordable food. Best of all, more and more destinations are offering year-round farmers' markets, and not just major cities like New York, Los Angeles, and San Francisco. You can find farmers' markets open year-round in cities like Greensboro, North Carolina; Houston; Tucson; Virginia Beach, Virginia; and hundreds of smaller communities around the country. Check out www.farmersmarket.com or www.localharvest.org to find open-air and covered markets by city and state, plus details on the season and times that they're open.

Los Angeles, California

Dates: January 25–30; February 1–6
Prices: $16.00–$28.00, for a three-course lunch; $26.00–$44.00 for a three-course dinner

After years of being outshone by New York, Los Angeles launched its own restaurant event, dineLA, in 2008. This event spans Los Angeles County from Pasadena to Malibu, Long Beach, and all points in between. There are three price points to choose from: deluxe (think Bubba Gump Shrimp), premier (like Katsuya in Hollywood), and fine dining (like Wolfgang Puck's Chinois on Main). Just think, you might find yourself dining next to a celebrity, and you don't even have to tell him or her you're eating off the prix fixe menu!

▶▶ www.dinela.com/restaurantweek

Baltimore, Maryland

Dates: January 23–February 1; July 31–August 9
Prices: $20.09 for a three-course lunch; $30.09 for a three-course dinner

Here's your chance to sample Maryland's famous crab cakes and much, much more. Typically, more than 100 restaurants participate in this event every year, meaning you can dine your way through Baltimore from Inner Harbor to Little Italy, Fells Point, and beyond.

▶▶ www.baltimorerestaurantweek.com

Philadelphia, Pennsylvania

Dates: January 25–30
Price: $35.00 for a three-course dinner

Though you can only take advantage of the prix fixe for dinner during Philadelphia's Center City District Restaurant Week, this event picks up steam each year. There are more than 100 participating restaurants, and patrons get discounted parking rates at multiple parking garages. For a real foodie experience, make your reservations at seafood guru Eric Ripert's 10 Arts.

▶▶ www.centercityphila.org/life/RestaurantWeek.php

Chicago, Illinois

Dates: February 20–27
Prices: $22.00 for a three-course lunch; $32.00 for a three-course dinner

Once known as a bratwurst, beer, and pizza kind of town, Chicago is now a top contender in the culinary scene. Chi-town's inaugural Restaurant Week in 2008 was such a hit that the number of participating restaurants has more than tripled for 2009, bringing the total up to about 150. Since the first year featured a lot of chains, this is great news for Chicago's local cuisine, which will surely be showcased in future events.

▶▶ www.choosechicago.com/eatitup

> **Tip:** Many cities host a "Taste Of" event each year, which allows you to sample the cuisine from scores of local restaurants, usually while enjoying live music, arts and crafts, and cooking demonstrations. In Chicago, the annual Taste Of event takes place in late June or early July and offers dishes from about 64 restaurants—you can get up to 6 tastings for $12.00. Denver's A Taste of Colorado takes place over Labor Day weekend and has everything from fried pickles to Colorado lamb. Atlanta's annual 2-day event in October features food from 70 restaurants.

Denver, Colorado

Dates: February 21–27
Price: $26.40 for a three-course dinner

A dinner for two at Denver's Restaurant Week will cost you only $52.80. Why? Because there are 5,280 feet in a mile, and Denver is known as the Mile-High City. The more than 200 participating restaurants include the Fort, which Bill Clinton chose to host a dinner for the G8 Summit; the restaurant claims to sell more buffalo steaks than any other independently owned restaurant in the country.

▶▶ www.denverrestaurantweek.com

Austin, Texas

Dates: March 1–4 and 8–11; August dates to be determined
Prices: $25.00 or $35.00 for a three-course dinner

Austin's foodie scene has been blossoming for some time now, and it's got a new Restaurant Week to prove it. Local high-end favorites include Aquarelle and Roaring Fork, a spin-off of a Phoenix-based restaurant.

▶▶ www.restaurantweekaustin.com

> **Tip:** How about having dinner in a secret, underground restaurant? Sounds intriguing, right? At underground restaurants, which are a kind of throwback to the old speakeasies, diners congregate to enjoy food in a secret location. They're unregulated, unlicensed, and, best of all, involve multicourse gourmet meals—often cooked by top-tier chefs—for a fraction of what you'd pay in a restaurant. The drawback is that it's difficult to base your travels around them because most are invite-only—meaning you have to send an e-mail and wait for a spot to open up. But if you're looking for a cool foodie experience in San Francisco, check out Ghetto Gourmet. One Pot is Seattle's underground restaurant, and Austin has the monthly Supper Underground, where you pay as much—or as little—as you want to.

Boston, Massachusetts

Dates: March 15–20 and 22–27; August dates to be determined
Prices: $15.09 for a two-course lunch; $20.09 for a three-course lunch; $33.09 for a three-course dinner

Boston's Restaurant Week, which includes more than 150 restaurants, has upped the ante with a new, even more affordable two-course lunch. And some of the participating restaurants are making these specials available on Saturday instead of limiting it to the standard Sunday-through-Friday-only deal.

▸▸ www.bostonusa.com/restaurantweek

Southern New Jersey

Dates: March 22–27; October dates to be determined
Price: $35.00 for a four-course dinner

Southern New Jersey doesn't want its Restaurant Week to be over-shadowed by New York City's or Philadelphia's, and by offering four courses instead of three, it's succeeding. Now entering its 5th year, the event prides itself on including more than 60 independently owned South Jersey establishments. It's been so successful that there are now two restaurant weeks per year.

▸▸ www.sjhotchefs.com/restweek

> Tip: Sometimes experiencing cheap local food is as easy as driving along a "food trail" from farm to farm to taste cheeses, jams, wines, and other local specialties. VTCheese.com maps out 39 different cheese makers along the Vermont Cheese Trail. A Sweet 'n' Salty Trail through Pennsylvania Dutch Country gets you to various pretzel and chocolate makers. And you can check out SonomaCounty.com for a map of more than 100 organic and family-owned farms throughout California's wine country.
>
> ▸▸ Sweet n' Salty Trail, www.padutchcountry.com/our_world/sweet_ and_salty_trail.asp

Pittsburgh, Pennsylvania

Dates: June and November dates to be determined
Prices: $25.00 for a three-course lunch; $35.00 for a three-course dinner

This Pittsburgh dining event has been such a hit that it's been expanded to two events a year. My advice? Skip the Spaghetti Warehouse chain, where you can easily find dinner for under

$35.00 any day of the week, and opt for a higher-end restaurant like Bistro 19 or the Carlton.

▶▶ www.pittsburghcelebrates.org/restweek.asp

> **Tip:** The rewards program at www.rewardsnetwork.com actually gets you cash back when you dine at a participating restaurant, bar, or club. We're talking 15 to 20 percent back on your credit or debit card after you dine.

Phoenix and Tucson, Arizona

Dates: September 19–25
Price: $29.00 for a three-course dinner

When it launched in 2008, Arizona Restaurant Week included only Phoenix-area restaurants, but it has since expanded to Tucson. Look for three-course meals at some of the best in the West, such as the Bourbon Steakhouse, Roaring Fork, and Sol y Sombra. Organizers make it easy to choose your restaurant by posting the prix fixe menus online.

▶▶ www.arizonarestaurantweek.com

> **Tip:** What better way to save on dining costs than to take advantage of a free meal? If you're traveling with kids, forgo your fine-dining aspirations and head straight to restaurants that offer kids-eat-free promotions. At participating Denny's restaurants, kids 10 and under eat free on Tuesdays and Saturdays from 4:00 p.m. to 10:00 p.m. At Lone Star Steakhouse & Saloon, buying one adult dinner gets you two free kid's meals all day on Tuesdays. Check out www.mykidseatfree.com to find ongoing promotions at restaurants listed by city and state. And none of them are fast-food joints!

CHAPTER 13

SHOULDER/OFF-SEASON TRAVEL

ONE OF THE BEST WAYS TO SAVE MONEY—even in a great economy—is to ignore peak-season travel. It's crowded and over-priced, and good service is, to be polite, a challenge to find. In a tough economy, the off-season becomes wildly affordable. But now, in many cases the shoulder season is equally affordable, offering huge savings. And here's the best part: In absolutely terrible economic times—like now—even the lowest prices are negotiable.

DESTINATION	PEAK	LOW	SHOULDER	TRAVEL ADVICE
Colorado mountain resorts	• July and August • Winter holidays (December 15 through January 3)	• April • Mid-November through mid-December	• Mid-February through March • May and June • September through early November	Fall and spring prices are up to a third off peak winter rates. For example, a standard room at Aspen's upscale Little Nell Hotel is $415.00 in fall, $995.00 in winter, $1,210.00 at Christmastime, and $660.00 in summer.
Caribbean	• Winter holidays (December 15 through January 3) • Post-holidays (January 4 through early April)	• June through August	• Mid-April through June • September through mid-December	Rates decrease as much as 60 percent in June, July, and August due to tropical storms and intense heat. And remember that hurricane season runs from June through November, so travel insurance is a must.
Hawaii	• June through August • Winter holidays (December 15 through January 3)	• Mid-January through early March	• Mid-March through May • September through November	The demise of airlines like Aloha and ATA means reduced service to Hawaii and higher costs. But while it may be expensive to get there, it can be affordable to stay, because hotels and resorts are dropping rates to entice visitors.

DESTINATION	PEAK	LOW	SHOULDER	TRAVEL ADVICE
Orlando	• March through April • Mid-June through mid-August • Winter holidays (December 15 through January 3)	• Mid- to late January • May • September through early December	• February • Late May through mid-June • Late August	One rule here: Orlando tourism is dependent upon school schedules. That means prices can vary within a matter of weeks. The Walt Disney World Dolphin hotel in mid-June starts at about $340.00, in mid-August it's $255.00, in late September it's about $220.00, and at Christmastime it's about $320.00.
New England	• September through late November • June through mid-August	• Mid-April through May	• Early January through March for snow and ski areas	New England is one of the few destinations that peaks in fall, particularly in October. To save on costs, consider an alternative fall-foliage destination such as Colorado, North Carolina, or the North Shore of Minnesota. And remember that ski resorts give as much as half off their winter rates in the spring and summer.
Las Vegas	• September through November • New Year's Eve • January through February • April through May	• June through August	• Fall, immediately before and after Thanksgiving	Vegas is scorchingly hot in the summer, but if you're hanging out on the Strip, chances are you won't spend much time outdoors. This is still a city of $50.00 hotel rooms and $8.95 buffets, so affordable stays are easy to come by—it's the casinos that will kill you.
Québec	• Late June through early September • Winter holidays (December 15 through January 3)	• November through mid-December • March through April	• May through mid-June • Mid-September through October	Because Canada doesn't celebrate Memorial Day, which is often the cusp between the shoulder and high seasons, you can find deals here. The Courtyard by Marriott in downtown Québec starts around $155.00 a night that weekend, compared with $209.00 over the weekend of July 4 (which Canadians also don't celebrate, but it happens to fall in their peak season).

DESTINATION	PEAK	LOW	SHOULDER	TRAVEL ADVICE
Mexican Riviera	• Mid-December through Easter	• July through August	• Mid-April through June • Late September through mid-December	Prices drop as much as 40 percent during the low season. Unfortunately, rainy weather and hurricanes can put a damper on your travels. However, you can find great post-holiday deals from early January through February.
Western Europe (Paris, Rome, London, Amsterdam, etc.)	• Late May through August (pre-Easter in Italy) • Winter holidays (December 15 through January 3)	• January through March	• April through mid-May • September through mid-November	These days, even shoulder season—traditionally a golden travel period in Europe—is pricey for most Americans. So bring a coat and travel to Europe in January. The three-star Hotel Trevi in Rome starts at €69.00 a night in mid-January versus €249.00 in mid-May and mid-September.
Central and Eastern Europe (Istanbul, Budapest, Sofia, etc.)	• Winter holidays (December 15 through January 3) • Mid-May through mid-August	• Late November through early December • Late August	• April through early May • September through mid-November	Though you can often save by traveling to this region rather than to Western Europe, the low season here can be pretty miserable, with bad weather and unpredictable hours for tourism-related businesses.
Costa Rica	• December through April	• May through mid-November	• May • September through early November	During the low season, rates are up to 25 percent cheaper, but don't be misled by brochures that call the rainy period between May and mid-November the "green season." It's just wet. The good news is that these rains tend to come in bursts, punctuated by hours of sunshine.

CHAPTER 14

BUS TRAVEL

I NEVER THOUGHT I'D SAY THIS, but capacity cuts by airlines, increases in operating and fuel costs, and the general state of the economy have combined to create a price and service vacuum on many trips less than 500 miles. And who—or what—has filled that vacuum? Small luxury jets? No. Carpooling? Hardly. Amtrak? Amtrak wishes. No, it's time to go back to the future. If you're going fewer than 500 miles and you're not in a hurry, the bus is the way to go.

Bus travel, surprisingly, has become an economically viable travel alternative. Not only can you save significantly compared with train and plane travel, but some bus companies are also becoming more upscale by providing amenities such as Wi-Fi and power outlets. It's not a bad experience overall if you can handle sitting upright for hours at a time.

Budget Buses

A $1.00 bus ticket? Usually I say if it sounds too good to be true, it is. And while that advertised $1.00 comes with a great big asterisk, today's discount buses are definite money savers, and they aren't nearly as shabby as you might expect.

Megabus, launched in 2006, serves the Midwest and the Northeast corridor up to Toronto at fares as low as $1.00. It used to service the West Coast, but quietly eliminated that route due to lack of demand.

But where it works, it really works. We're talking nonstop service between 17 cities in the Midwest and 12 in the Northeast, guaranteed seating on single and double-decker buses, power outlets at each seat on the new double-decker buses, and free Wi-Fi.

Those $1.00 tickets are limited to just a few seats per ride, but the rule of thumb is the earlier you book, the more you save. Even if the $1.00 tickets aren't available, the price goes up incrementally, so you might still pay just a few bucks each way. However, if you buy a ticket within 24 hours of departure, expect to pay up to $85.00 one-way.

And travelers have been paying attention: Megabus reported that its sales shot up 225 percent between October 2007 and October 2008.

Some of the most popular Megabus routes are Minneapolis; St. Louis, Missouri; and Indianapolis to Chicago on the Midwest route, and Washington, DC; Baltimore; Philadelphia; and Boston to New York City in the Northeast.

BoltBus, a division of Greyhound, covers the New York City to Washington, DC, route, with stops in Philadelphia and Cherry Hill, New Jersey. Buses also run between Boston and New York City. Launched in 2008, it quickly became a strong competitor among the Northeast corridor transportation options, which include Amtrak's Acela Express and shuttle airplane services from Delta and US Airways. It, too, offers $1 fares and comes equipped with Wi-Fi and power outlets and boasts 3 extra inches of legroom (BoltBus had to remove seats to make that happen).

Another inexpensive option is to travel by **Greyhound,** which has been servicing the United States and Canada since 1914. In some major cutbacks in 2004, the bus line removed less profitable routes to focus on more profitable ones such as the Northeast corridor—bad news for rural areas, but good news for those who travel the more popular routes.

Want to know how competitive buses are? Just look at these comparisons of one-way fares, booked about 3 weeks in advance (lowest fare and minimum travel time reported; flights are all nonstop, and prices do not include taxes and fees).

New York to DC

Megabus: $8.00; 4 hours, 30 minutes

BoltBus: $15.00; 4 hours, 15 minutes

Greyhound: $35.00; 4 hours, 20 minutes

Amtrak (Acela Express): $72.00; 4 hours

JetBlue (JFK to Dulles): $64.00; 1 hour, 30 minutes

Delta Shuttle (LaGuardia to Reagan): $64.00; about 1 hour

US Airways Shuttle (LaGuardia to Reagan): $64.00; about 1 hour

Minneapolis to Chicago

Megabus: $25.00; 8 hours

Greyhound: $61.00; 8 hours, 25 minutes

Amtrak: $74.00; 8 hours, 5 minutes

American Airlines (Minneapolis-St. Paul to O'Hare): $474.00 ($376.00 round-trip); 1 hour, 25 minutes

Northwest (Minneapolis-St. Paul to O'Hare): $396.00 ($350.00 round-trip); 1 hour, 22 minutes

United (Minneapolis-St. Paul to O'Hare): $436.00 ($349.00 round-trip); 1 hour, 18 minutes

New York to Toronto

Megabus: $45.00; 10 hours

Greyhound: $85.00; 10 hours, 15 minutes

Amtrak: $96.00; 12 hours, 30 minutes

American Airlines (JFK to Pearson): $70.00 ($166.00 round-trip); 1 hour, 45 minutes

Delta (JFK to Pearson): $96.00 ($193.00 round-trip); 1 hour, 45 minutes

Memphis to Dallas

Greyhound: $80.00; 8 hours, 5 minutes

Amtrak: $201.00; 32 hours, 35 minutes

American Airlines (Memphis to Dallas-Fort Worth): $589.00 ($196.00 round-trip); 1 hour, 45 minutes

Los Angeles to Las Vegas

Greyhound: $39.00; 4 hours, 50 minutes

Amtrak (bus service): $38.00; 5 hours, 50 minutes

Southwest (LAX to McCarran): $139.00 ($258.00 round-trip); 1 hour, 5 minutes 8

Philadelphia to Atlantic City

Greyhound: $11.50; 1 hour, 16 minutes

Amtrak: $8; 1 hour, 36 minutes

Besides the fact that buses are at the mercy of traffic jams, one of the biggest drawbacks of traveling by bus is that you must travel light. If you have more than one piece of luggage, the operator can refuse it, leaving you (or just your bag) stranded at the bus stop. And, in the case of BoltBus, if you have a complaint, there is no customer service number to call; part of the reason it can offer discount prices is that it's run only online, so there's little overhead.

▶▶ Megabus: www.megabus.com, www.megabus.com/uk

▶▶ BoltBus: www.boltbus.com

▶▶ Greyhound: www.greyhound.com

Canada

Fortunately, traveling by bus in Canada is pretty much the same as it is here in the United States. **Greyhound Canada** is the country's largest service. If you're a visitor trying to get from Toronto to Vancouver, a 2-day bus ride probably isn't in your best interest. And, between major destinations, Canada's national rail system, VIA Rail, can actually beat bus travel in terms of value and time. (All routes are one-way unless otherwise noted; lowest fare—in US dollars—and minimum travel time reported; flights are nonstop.)

Edmonton to Vancouver

Greyhound: $103.00; 16 hours, 45 minutes

VIA Rail: $95.00 (supersaver fare); 27 hours, 5 minutes

Air Canada (Edmonton to Vancouver): $72.00 ($183.00 round-trip); 40 minutes

Toronto to Montreal

Greyhound: $95.00; 7 hours, 50 minutes

VIA Rail: $64.00 (supersaver fare); 4 hours, 33 minutes

Air Canada (Air Jazz) (Toronto to Trudeau): $72.00 ($144.00 round-trip); 1 hour, 15 minutes

▶▶ Greyhound Canada: www.greyhound.ca

Europe

As much as we'd like to think of the United States as the pioneer of all great ideas, we appropriated the budget bus concept from Europe. **Megabus** originated in the United Kingdom in 2003, where one or two £1 fares are still available on most routes. Even though the United Kingdom's train system is famously efficient, Megabus just keeps growing. London to Liverpool? Ten pounds. London to Edinburgh, Scotland? Twelve pounds. You can't beat that.

But Megabus isn't the only budget bus company around. Affordable coach travel is possible throughout much of Europe—you just have to plan ahead and expect to spend a good chunk of your time sitting in rather cramped quarters. Think of it as an opportunity to get to know the locals.

Eurolines is Europe's largest budget bus option. It's actually a consortium of 32 independent bus companies from across the continent. So a Eurolines bus in the United Kingdom, which operates under the National Express brand, is connected with different service than Eurolines Bulgaria, but they all operate under a similar standard of quality.

A Eurolines pass offers unlimited travel between 35 cities in 16 countries. A 15-day adult pass costs £139 to £229 (about $207.00 to $342.00), and a 30-day pass is £209 to £299 (about $312.00 to $447.00), depending on the season. You'll find the best deals from early January through mid-March and from November through the 2nd week in December. Youth passes for travelers age 26 and under are about £20 cheaper.

As for point-to-point travel, the best option depends on what's important to you: budget, expediency, or comfort. Say you want to travel one-way from Paris to Barcelona in the spring. You have three affordable options: bus, train, and plane (a one-way car rental is usually prohibitively expensive due to drop-off fees).

Eurolines (bus): about $89.00; 19 hours, 45 minutes
Rail Europe (train): about $112.00; 11 hours, 52 minutes
Vueling (airplane): about $90.00; 1 hour, 45 minutes

When you look at the numbers, it seems like flying is your best bet, right? It's quicker and cheaper than the bus or train. But you have to take into consideration the experience. The Paris and Barcelona airports are outside their city centers, which means you'll have to take the metro, a bus, or a taxi out there. Vueling also charges €10 (about $13.00) for luggage up to 20 kilograms (about 40 pounds), and €8 (approximately $10.00) for every kilo after that.

Now, my vote would be for the train—you'll save on hotel costs if you take an overnight trip, and you can sit back and enjoy the view while drinking a glass of wine. But for budget travelers, the bus wins every time.

▶▶ Eurolines: www.eurolines.com

South America

In South America, going by bus is one of the cheapest ways to get around, and most major cities have at least one terminal serving long-distance routes.

In **Buenos Aires, Argentina,** chances are you'll depart from Terminal de Ómibus de Retiro (or just Retiro). There, you can connect with dozens of bus companies that will take you all through Argentina and even into parts of Chile. There are usually two types of service: *semi cama,* which means you'll get a reclining seat, a meal, and maybe a movie, and *coche cama,* which has roomier seats, a movie, a meal, and fewer stops.

For example, the trip from Buenos Aires to the Terminal del Sol station in Mendoza might cost about $35.00 for *semi cama,* while *coche cama* is about $45.00. Just remember to pack your iPod—it's a 13-hour ride.

The Retiro Web site is in Spanish, but you can easily buy tickets at the bus station or ticket offices throughout the city. Book in advance if you're traveling during the peak summer months, from January to March.

In **Bolivia,** long-distance buses are called *flotas,* and you'll find plenty of dirt-cheap options from La Paz to major destinations such as Oruro, Copacabana, Sucre, and Santa Cruz.

Keep in mind that while roads between major cities are generally well maintained, things can get rough when heading into the Andes, where roads are narrow, winding, and have steep drop-offs. Consider this scary fact: Until a new road was constructed a few years ago, the only route between La Paz and Coroico was the

Some General Tips on Safety

- Be smart. Bus stations can be hotspots for opportunistic thieves and pickpockets. Be aware of your surroundings and don't wear flashy jewelry or open your wallet in public.

- Traveling at night is a good way to save on hotel costs, but it's not necessarily the safest option. In the winter, especially in the mountainous areas, roads can be icy and slippery. Nighttime travel also makes you more vulnerable to theft and pickpocketing.

- Bus drivers in South America are perceived as notoriously reckless. The trade off here is that the price is right, but try to sit at the back of the bus near the rear exit, just in case!

- Verify where your destination bus terminal is located and don't get off the bus anywhere but at an official terminal. The US Embassy in La Paz has received reports of US citizens traveling in the evening by bus from Copacabana to La Paz being kidnapped and robbed. The crimes can happen easily because bus drivers sometimes stop short of the La Paz bus terminal, usually around the General Cemetery, and thieves strike when the tourists are trying to hail a taxi.

single-lane, two-way North Yungas Road, which hugs the side of a mountain and was dubbed "the world's most dangerous road."

The main bus terminal in La Paz is located on Plaza Antofagasta at Avenida Uruguay, about a 4-minute taxi ride from the city center.

Rio de Janeiro, Brazil, not only has an excellent inner-city bus system, but you can also easily travel around the entire country via bus. All long-distance buses depart from Rodoviária Novo Rio on Avenida Francisco Bicalho. For just a few dollars, you can travel from Rio de Janeiro to other major Brazilian destinations such as São Paulo, Vitória, and Salvador, and even into Buenos Aires.

Santiago, Chile, has four major bus terminals: Terminal Alameda, Terminal Los Héroes, Terminal San Borja, and Terminal Santiago. Two of the major Chilean bus companies you'll want to seek out are **Tur Bus** and **Pullman,** both of which depart from Terminal Alameda.

So, for example, if you were headed to Mendoza, Argentina, you could hop on either bus line for about $15.00 to $20.00 for a 6-hour journey. Take my advice and do the trip in the daytime— the views are breathtaking.

▶▶Terminal de Ómibus de Retiro (Buenos Aires): www.tebasa.com.ar (in Spanish)

▶▶Rodoviária Novo Rio (Rio de Janeiro): www.novorio.com.br (in Portuguese)

▽ Additional Resources:

US State Department tips on driving overseas: http://travel.state.gov/travel/tips/safety/safety_1179.html

CHAPTER 15

TRAIN TRAVEL

IN THE UNITED STATES, Amtrak has been an embarrassment on many fronts, including that it is not truly a high-speed rail line, its terrible on-time performance, and its inability to market itself properly. At the opposite end of the spectrum is the rail system in Europe, where traveling by train is so efficient that it's practically become a rite of passage. Or, put more simply, it's passage done right. And, considering the frequent flight delays worldwide, train travel has also become a viable option in countries you may not have considered visiting before, and in countries you might have considered prohibitively expensive to visit.

But now, it's a win-win. You can save money using the train, and you get to go to places that were once too expensive. The deals are definitely out there and, as the world continues its financial meltdown, taking the train makes economic sense and reduces the stress of getting to and from airports, checking luggage, and waiting in long lines at security checkpoints.

In many cases, both in the United States and abroad, buying rail passes will save you money in a number of ways. For the most part, on a per-mile basis, traveling the rails costs substantially less than flying or renting a car—and, considering what foreigners pay for gas (prices are more than $10 a gallon in England), you definitely don't want to rent a car. And second, if you plan correctly, trains can save you money on hotels if you schedule late-night departures. Lastly, many overseas rail passes are priced in US dollars, so they are also an effective hedge against rising exchange rates.

Amtrak Rail Passes

Here's something you may not have known: **Amtrak** has rail passes, too. Sometimes I'm not sure if Amtrak even knows that. The train may not always be on time, but with a rail pass, the price is definitely right. (General rule of thumb: Long-haul Amtrak journeys, like the Texas Eagle from Chicago to Los Angeles, tend to arrive on time pretty much never. Routes like the Acela Express from Washington, DC, to Boston, and the Hiawatha from Milwaukee to Chicago tend to be on time at least 85 percent of the time.)

Until recently, the **USA Rail Pass** was available for purchase only outside of the country, but now it's also an option for American travelers. It lets you ride the rails anywhere in the continental United States for a 15-, 30-, or 45-day period. It's not hop-on-hop-off, though; you have to make a reservation by phone or online for each leg of your journey, but the fare is included in the cost of your pass.

But there is one catch: Each pass has a fixed number of "segments," or legs: 8 for the 15-day, 12 for the 30-day, and 18 for the 45-day pass. Each time you get on and then get off a vehicle (whether it's a train or a connecting bus or ferry) is considered a segment. So, taking a trip from Washington, DC, to Oklahoma City would count as at least three segments, because you'd have to change trains in Chicago and in Fort Worth, Texas.

In addition, the high-speed Acela service and any Canadian routes jointly operated by Amtrak and Canada's VIA Rail aren't included in the deal. Remember, too, that when it comes to Amtrak and "high speed," you need to put things in perspective. For example, from New York to Washington, DC, the Acela can cost $133.00 to $177.00 each way. But the Northeast Regional service, which costs $72.00 to $102.00 each way, takes only

40 minutes to 1 hour and 10 minutes longer, depending on the schedule. And that presumes the Acela is on time!

> ### 📍 Amtrak Rail Pass
>
> 15 days, 8 segments: $389.00
> 30 days, 12 segments: $579.00
> 45 days, 18 segments: $749.00
>
> ▶▶ 800-USA-RAIL, http://tickets.amtrak.com/itd/amtrak/selectpass

Another Amtrak option is the **California Rail Pass,** which costs $159.00 for 7 days of travel over a 21-day period. Admittedly, this deal will appeal only to those who want to traverse California, but the best way to really experience this state is by train.

With this pass, you get access to:

Capitol Corridor, which takes you from San Jose through Oakland, Berkeley, and Sacramento and ends in Auburn

San Joaquin Corridor, which takes you through the Central Valley, from Bakersfield to Modesto, Merced, Fresno, and Sacramento

Pacific Surfliner (my favorite), which takes you up the coast from San Diego to Los Angeles, Santa Barbara, and San Luis Obispo

Coast Starlight, which runs from Los Angeles to Santa Barbara, Salinas, San Jose, Oakland, Sacramento, and up to Dunsmuir

▶▶ Amtrak: www.amtrak.com

Europe
Although the rise of European budget airlines has introduced some competition, train travel still has undeniable benefits. First, train stations are usually located close to the city center, while

airports tend to be on the outskirts—consider Ryanair, for example, which flies in and out of Stansted Airport, about 25 miles from London. In addition, budget carriers have strict rules about luggage—EasyJet, for example, sets a limit of 20 kilograms (44 pounds) per passenger for checked bags and charges about $10.00 for every kilogram over. And if your carry-on is larger than 21 by 15 by 7.5 inches, guess what? You're going to have to check it, and pay for the excess weight. With trains, you bring as much as you can carry for no extra charge.

Most people think Eurail Passes are only for students wearing the mandatory pair of Birkenstocks, but that's no longer the case. The **Eurail Pass,** sold only to non-Europeans, has come a long way since the days of kids backpacking through 20 countries in 15 days. Not only can you buy all-inclusive Europe-wide passes good for 2-week to 3-month periods, you can also buy regional and single-country passes to fit your travel plans.

However, although Eurail is perhaps the most popular resource for purchasing rail passes, you can also go directly to the source, **Rail Europe,** for even more options, such as a France-only pass or point-to-point tickets.

A general rule of thumb is that if you're taking more than one point-to-point train journey, you'll get a better value with a rail pass. You also won't be as committed to a specific timetable, so you can hop on and hop off whenever you want.

Which Pass Is Best?

Visiting more than 5 countries: Global Pass, valid in 20 countries

Visiting 3 to 5 countries: Select Pass, valid in 3 to 5 bordering countries

Visiting 2 countries: Regional Pass, valid in 2 of 25 regions

Visiting 1 country: One-Country Pass

Despite all the options Eurail Passes now offer, the 20-countries-in-15-days mentality still holds sway with the younger crowd. According to STA Travel, a travel-booking agency geared toward students, the most popular rail pass it sells is the second-class youth **Global Pass,** which can be used to travel in 20 participating countries.

If you're over age 25, you can still save if you buddy up. Eurail knocks an average of 17 percent off the regular fare when two or more people travel together. With the 15-day Global Pass, you save about 15 percent, or $110.00.

Global Passes

For 15-day passes, the youth Global Pass, which is only for travelers under age 26, starts around $475.00 and the adult Global Pass starts around $729.00. The participating countries are Austria, Belgium, Croatia, Denmark, Finland, France, Germany, Greece, Hungary, Ireland, Italy, Luxembourg, the Netherlands, Norway, Portugal, Romania, Slovenia, Spain, Sweden, and Switzerland.

> **Tip:** If you want to stretch your dollar further, take the train to Hungary or Croatia. To date, they still haven't adopted the euro as their currency and so they tend to be a lot more affordable than Western Europe. (But don't expect many high-speed trains on this journey.)

Single-Country Passes

Single-country passes can be an economical way to explore a country's nooks and crannies without having to deal with the hassles of renting a car and navigating your way through unfamiliar streets.

The **Eurail Italy** pass, for example, is good for unlimited rail travel in Italy, though you have to make advance reservations and pay a small fee to ride certain high-speed trains (such as ES* Italia), couchettes, and sleepers, which are noted with an R in timetables and at stations. Traveling first-class for 6 days within a 2-month

> **Tip:** Should you travel first-class or second-class? While a second-class ticket is always cheaper, consider what kind of experience you're looking for. A first-class ticket allows you to travel in cars for either class. So if you're in the mood to meet locals and other travelers, you can head for the second-class area; if you want privacy, sleep, and air-conditioning, walk up to first class. In most cases, you won't even have a choice: Many adult passes are available only for first-class (leaving the second-class option for travelers under age 26). But for comparison, the cheapest France-Italy adult pass from Rail Europe is $320.00 for second-class and $367.00 for first.

period will cost about $316.00. With your other option being to fly between cities via Alitalia, well, the choice is clear.

Other One-Country Passes available through Eurail and/or Rail Europe let you travel in Austria, Croatia, Czech Republic, Denmark, Finland, France, Greece, Holland, Hungary, Ireland, Norway, Poland, Portugal, Romania, Slovenia, Spain, and Sweden.

Unless you're really into a country's culture (or you're touring with a band), some countries just aren't worth getting a single-country pass for. Take Greece, for example. A Greece-only rail pass that gives you more than 4 days of travel in a 1-month period will cost at least $189.00. Sure, you can take the train from Athens to Thessaloniki and then . . . well, that's about it. No ferries, no island-hopping. Instead, your better bet is a Greece-Italy Pass, which starts at $289.00 and includes ferry service between the two countries.

And that opens up a whole new category of travel.

Regional Passes

In broad terms, a regional pass is perhaps my favorite option for exploring Europe on a budget: You get up-close access to a region, and you're not forced to pack in the entire continent in under a month. France-Spain, France-Italy, Austria-Croatia/Slovenia, Finland-Sweden: The possibilities are practically limitless.

▶▶ Rail Europe: 800-438-7245, www.raileurope.com

▶▶ Eurail: 800-722-7151, www.eurail.com

Australia

Australia is so huge I often recommend that travelers take the train to experience the country. The good news is that it's catching on, and as a result **Rail Australia** has developed several types of passes for different itineraries.

To start, there are several long-haul train routes: the Indian Pacific line from Sydney to Perth via Adelaide, the Ghan from Adelaide to Darwin via Alice Springs, the Overland from Melbourne to Adelaide, and Queensland Rail from Brisbane to Townsville and Cairns. The shorter-haul CountryLink routes run from Sydney to Melbourne, Canberra, and Brisbane.

For the average traveler, the best bet is the **Backtracker Pass,** which for AU$232.00 (about $152.00) gives you 14 days of access to the CountryLink routes. Compare with flying from point to point on budget carrier Virgin Blue, which charges about $180.00 for a flexible ticket from Melbourne to Sydney

Another option is the **East Coast Discovery Pass,** which offers unlimited travel one-way in New South Wales and Queensland. The cost depends on your start and end points, but you're looking at AU$500.50 (about $329.00) to travel from Melbourne all the way up to Cairns. A flexible Virgin Blue ticket is AU$275.00 (about $180.00), so while you're not saving much, you do have the option to hop on and off the train to explore points in between.

For more adventurous types, the longer-haul routes have their own options. The **Rail Explorer Pass** costs AU$690.00 (about $453.00) and is valid for 6 months. It gives you unlimited access on the Ghan, Indian Pacific, and Overland lines.

The **Austrail Flexi Pass** lets you travel on all the participating lines. You can get either 15 or 22 days of travel during a 6-month period at a cost of AU$950.00 and AU$1330.00 (about $625.00 and $875.00, respectively). Passes are available for purchase only outside Australia.

▶▶ Rail Australia: www.railaustralia.com.au

Canada

VIA Rail is the Canadian equivalent of Amtrak, and if you're looking to travel around Canada, the train is the best way to get around while enjoying some spectacular scenery.

Unfortunately, the North American Rail Pass that once allowed travel on both Amtrak and VIA Rail is no longer available. The most comprehensive rail pass—and I really like this one for both business and leisure travel—is the **Canrailpass,** which gives you unlimited travel on any VIA train for 12 days over a 30-day period. The price ranges from $549.00 to $879.00, depending on the season.

If you don't have quite that much time to spend traversing Canada, check out the **Corridorpass,** which gives you 10 days of travel in southern Québec and southern Ontario. It gets you access to major tourist destinations such as Québec City, Toronto, and Niagara Falls at a price that starts at $314.00.

▶▶ VIA Rail: www.viarail.ca

▽ Additional Resources:

The Man in Seat Sixty-One: www.seat61.com

> Tip: Take the 3-day journey on the Canadian from Toronto to Vancouver via the Rocky Mountains. A first-class sleeper car will cost you about $700.00, and it's worth every dime. (Or, if you can handle sitting upright for those 3 days, an economy ticket is about $200.00.) In comparison, a one-way flight on Air Canada runs from about $130.00 to $450.00 (and more than $1,300.00 for "executive class"). But by opting for expediency over experience, you'll miss out on the view, the social aspect, and, in many cases, Wi-Fi access and power outlets.

CHAPTER 16

TRAVEL-FRIENDLY CREDIT CARDS

I'M SURE YOU'VE SEEN IT HAPPEN. You come home from an international trip and, a month later, there's a nasty surprise in your credit card statement. Every purchase you made, even if you went only as far as Canada, has an extra charge attached to it—something called a foreign-transaction or conversion fee. This is a standard 1 percent fee that Visa and MasterCard charge on all purchases made in foreign currency to cover the cost of converting the charge into US dollars.

That's bad enough. But then the bank that issued your credit card adds on its own transaction fee, often as high as 3 percent. And don't think you can avoid these fees by using your ATM card to withdraw local currency—many banks will charge you a percentage, a flat fee, or both to take out money abroad. When they levy a percentage fee, banks usually make their calculations after the charge has been converted into US dollars—so the amount you pay is affected by the current currency conversion rate.

Capital One does perhaps the best job of marketing itself as a travel-friendly credit and debit card provider, and with good reason—not only does it not charge you that unpleasant foreign-transaction fee or an ATM withdrawal fee, it also swallows the 1 percent conversion fee from Visa and MasterCard. But just because a bank does a good job advertising doesn't mean it's the only option out there: First Republic, Charles Schwab, and Washington Mutual are also top choices for travelers.

We checked in with other credit card companies and banks and, along with our friends at Bankrate.com, we figured out who is charging what to overseas travelers.

Some things to keep in mind:

1. Even if a bank doesn't charge a foreign-transaction fee for credit card usage, in most cases, you'll still see that 1 percent fee levied by Visa and MasterCard.

2. If your issuing bank charges no ATM withdrawal fee, you may still end up paying a fee levied by the bank you're withdrawing the money from.

American Express

Credit card foreign-transaction fee: 2.7 percent

Debit card foreign-transaction fee: not available for foreign use

ATM foreign-transaction fee: 3 percent with a minimum withdrawal of $5.00 (Cardmembers must be enrolled in the Express Cash feature prior to traveling or using the ATM.)

Bank of America

Credit card foreign-transaction fee: 3 percent

Debit card foreign-transaction fee: 3 percent

ATM foreign-transaction fee: $5.00 fee plus 1 percent of ATM withdrawal. However, these fees are waived for customers withdrawing from ATM alliance members: Barclays (United Kingdom), BNP Paribas (France), Deutsche Bank (Germany), Scotiabank (Canada), and Westpac (Australia and New Zealand). In addition, as a result of other partnerships, the fees are also waived at China Construction Bank (China) and Santander Serfin (Mexico). Note that the fee is waived only in each bank's home country—so if you use a Deustche Bank outside of Germany, for example, you may be charged.

BB&T

Credit card foreign-transaction fee: 2 percent

Debit card foreign-transaction fee: 2 percent
ATM foreign-transaction fee: $2.00 fee plus 2 percent

☝Capital One

Credit card foreign-transaction fee: zero percent
Debit card foreign-transaction fee: zero percent
ATM foreign-transaction fee: zero percent (A fee will be
    assessed when using a non-Capital One ATM, which is
    also their policy if you use a non-Capital One ATM in
    the United States.)

Not only does Capital One not levy any fees, it also absorbs the
1 percent fee charged by Visa and MasterCard.

☝Charles Schwab

Credit card foreign-transaction fee: zero percent
Debit card foreign-transaction fee: zero percent
ATM foreign-transaction fee: zero percent

Here's an interesting benefit: If you have a Schwab High-Yield
Investor checking account and use your Schwab Bank Platinum
Check Card to withdraw cash from an ATM, the bank will actually reimburse you for any ATM fees you incur on your travels.
This doesn't apply to ATM transactions other than cash with-
drawals (like checking your balance or buying stamps) or to the 1
percent currency-exchange fee levied by Visa and MasterCard.

Chase

Credit card foreign-transaction fee: 3 percent
Debit card foreign-transaction fee: 3 percent
ATM foreign-transaction fee: 3 percent after currency
    conversion, plus a $3.00 charge for withdrawing money
    from a non-Chase ATM outside of the United States.
    Chase Premier Platinum checking account customers are
    exempt from that $3.00 charge.

Citibank

    Credit card foreign-transaction fee: 3 percent

    Debit card foreign-transaction fee: 3 percent (The fee is waived for Citigold customers)

    ATM foreign-transaction fee: 3 percent plus a $1.50 charge for a withdrawal from a non-Citibank ATM (These fees are waived for Citigold customers)

👍Commerce Bank

    Credit card foreign-transaction fee: not applicable

    Debit card foreign-transaction fee: zero percent

    ATM foreign-transaction fee: zero percent

This Pennsylvania-based bank not only ended ATM surcharges worldwide in 2005, it also began reimbursing the fees imposed by other banks—in effect making every ATM a no-fee ATM. The catch is that the fee is waived only if you have a minimum daily balance of $2,500.00 in your account with the bank. Everyone else is subject to an extra charge.

👍Discover

    Credit card foreign-transaction fee: zero percent

    Debit card foreign-transaction fee: not applicable

    ATM foreign-transaction fee: not applicable

Though the zero percent foreign conversion rate is great, the big drawback here is that the Discover card isn't widely accepted outside of the United States.

👍First Republic Bank

    Credit card foreign-transaction fee: zero percent

    Debit card foreign-transaction fee: zero percent

    ATM foreign-transaction fee: zero percent

First Republic will also reimburse the ATM access fees imposed by other financial institutions. (A $2,500 minimum checking account balance is required.)

HSBC

Credit card foreign-transaction fee: 3 percent (no fee for HSBC Premier World MasterCard cardholders)

Debit card foreign-transaction fee: 3 percent (zero percent for HSBC Premier Debit MasterCard cardholders)

ATM foreign-transaction fee: 3 percent (zero percent for HSBC Premier Debit MasterCard cardholders)

❦SunTrust

Credit card foreign-transaction fee: 3 percent (1 percent for SunTrust Signature Credit cardholders)

Debit card foreign-transaction fee: 3 percent

ATM foreign-transaction fee: 3 percent plus a $5.00 fee

Wachovia

Credit card foreign-transaction fee: 3 percent

Debit card foreign-transaction fee: 2 percent

ATM foreign-transaction fee: 2 percent

👍Washington Mutual

Credit card foreign-transaction fee: 1 percent

Debit card foreign-transaction fee: 3 percent

ATM foreign-transaction fee: 1 percent, plus a $2.00 fee (Fee is waived for Washington Mutual Free Checking account holders.)

👎Wells Fargo

Credit card foreign-transaction fee: 3 percent

Debit card foreign-transaction fee: 3 percent

ATM foreign-transaction fee: $5.00 fee per withdrawal

CHAPTER 17

PASSPORTS

THE TRUE DEFINITION of luxury travel, no matter what the economic conditions, is getting to keep your options open. And it's never been more important for you to have a passport, because when fares go down—and they will as demand shrinks—you'll have the option to travel anywhere. Having a passport enables you to immediately take advantage of a buyer's market in travel.

First, the Rules

Your passport must have at least two blank visa pages and be valid for at least 6 months after your date of departure. Otherwise, you may not be allowed to board your flight or reenter the United States. And remember, you now need a passport to return to the United States by air from Canada, Mexico, or the Caribbean. And as of June 2009, you'll also need one to return by land and sea. No matter where you're going, you don't want to put off getting a passport until the last minute. Here's why.

It takes anywhere from 3 to 8 weeks for the State Department to process your application. (When it was announced that passports would be required for reentry after land, sea, and air travel, it caused a 3-month backlog.) Then, there's the money. Let's start with the basic cost of a passport: $100.00 for a new adult passport (a $75.00 application fee and a $25.00 "execution fee," because it must be done in person) or $75.00 for a renewal (which is done by mail), plus the cost of the approved photos.

> **Tip:** If you're getting your passport for the first time, you have to appear in person and show a certified copy of your birth certificate. If you have your original birth certificate on hand, you'll save yourself the cost of having a service mail you a certified copy, which can run about $25.00, plus the shipping costs. And if you're in a hurry, that delivery fee will be costly.

If you have to expedite your application through the government, it gets really expensive. Not only will you have to pay the standard application fee of $75.00, you'll also have to pay an extra $60.00 for the rush, plus the additional cost for expedited delivery of both your application materials and the issued passport.

A dedicated expediting service can be your best friend if you need a passport or visa fast, but it's going to cost you. The faster you need it, the higher the service fee is.

There are several passport expediting services out there, but the one I use the most is It's Easy. Like most services, It's Easy has different tiers of payment for passport processing, depending on how fast you need it. (All time periods are in business days.)

Same business day—$249.00
2 to 4 days—$179.00
5 to 7 days—$129.00
8 to 10 days—$99.00
11 or more days—$65.00

▶▶ It's Easy, www.itseasy.com

Get it? Procrastinate now, pay later.

And the same goes for visas. Tourist visa fees and processes vary by country. If you're traveling to Australia, for example, you can apply online for $64.95, but if you're going to India, you have to mail in your passport, passport-sized photos, and payment of $73.00 for a 6-month visa. And those are just the base prices; if you're in a hurry, expect to pay a lot more.

But there are ways to save money on getting a passport.

Don't get stuck at the airport without the proper entry requirements. Check with the State Department for individual country requirements and fees.

▶▶ travel.state.gov

Take Your Own Photo

With today's technology, it's actually possible to take your own passport or visa photo.

One big caveat: There is a lot of room for error, so don't attempt this if you're in a hurry.

The State Department has a set of guidelines:

1. Frame subject with full face, front view, eyes open.
2. Make sure photo presents full head from top of hair to bottom of chin; height of head should measure 1 to 1⅜ inches (25 to 35 mm).
3. Center head within frame.
4. Make sure eye height is between 1⅛ to 1⅜ inches (28 and 35 mm) from bottom of photo.
5. Photograph subject against a plain white or off-white background.
6. Position subject and lighting so that there are no distracting shadows on the face or background.
7. Encourage subject to have a natural expression.

Confused yet?

The good news is that there are now free online services to help you get a photo of the right dimensions. I used ePassport Photo.com for a visa, and it processed without any problems. These services give you a 2-by-2-inch frame to position your uploaded photo correctly.

Best of all, you can print the picture on photo paper at home, for free. Or the service will validate that the photo meets all the necessary guidelines and mail you a set of six photos on passport-quality paper for about $6.00. Compare that with Federal Express Office (formerly Kinko's), which charges $12.95 for two pictures, and a photo shop that charges $12.95 for four.

▶▶ Passport photo guidelines, travel.state.gov/passport/guide/ guide_2081.html

▶▶ ePassportPhoto.com, www.epassportphoto.com

Don't Lose Your Passport!

If you lose your passport, there's no getting around paying the standard $100.00 renewal fee (except in special circumstances when you can't get the money before continuing travel). But you can make the process a lot easier, and save yourself valuable time, if you keep the information it contains safe.

Scan or photocopy your passport so you have a copy to show the US Embassy if you lose it on the road. If you're not comfortable traveling with a hard copy or a portable hard drive containing the image, e-mail yourself your scanned passport or store the image on a secure online site. Keepyousafe.com is a free site that allows you to store your vital travel documents. (If you run out of storage space, you can upgrade for $4.00 a month.)

▶▶ Online passport storage, www.keepyousafe.com

Passport Cards

The government recently began issuing passport cards, which are cheaper and smaller (about the size of a credit card) versions of the traditional passport. Most people don't need these cards or the extra expense, but frequent border crossers may want to take note.

The passport card facilitates the entry process at US land and sea ports of entry when arriving from Canada, Mexico, and the Caribbean, including Bermuda. First-time applicants pay $45.00 for an adult and $35.00 for a child under the age of 16; adults who already have a regular passport book issued within the past 15 years can get the card for $20.00. The idea is to let frequent border crossers use this cheaper card instead of carrying their traditional passport books back and forth. And if it gets lost, the replacement fee is only $20.00, not $75.00.

US Customs and Border Protection also offers special passport cards as part of the Trusted Traveler Program. These cards give you access to dedicated commuter lanes so you can skip the long lines at customs checkpoints. But not just anyone can get them—you have to go through a background check, fingerprinting, and an interview. If you frequently cross the US-Mexico border, you'll apply for a SENTRI card, which costs about $120.00. To travel to and from Canada, the NEXUS card will cost you about $50.00.

▶▶ **US Customs and Border Protection Trusted Traveler Program,** http://cbp.gov/xp/cgov/travel/trusted_traveler/

▽ Additional Resources:

US Department of State passport information, http://travel.state. gov/passport

Travel Industry Association passport help page, www.getapassportnow.com

CHAPTER 18

LUGGAGE

I HAVE A VERY SPECIFIC PHILOSOPHY when it comes to luggage: There are only two kinds of airline bags—carry-on and *lost*.

And I fondly remember the good old days when airlines used to lose my luggage for free. Wasn't that wonderful? Today, most of them want to charge for that service.

Airlines are doing everything they possibly can to raise revenue without officially raising fares, but when it comes to luggage, these new baggage fees have degenerated into an almost full-fledged war on consumers. Who wants to pay up to $75.00 (depending upon weight) to check two bags on a one-way flight? For a family of four, this could add an extra $600.00 to the roundtrip ticket cost.

If you're checking bags, read this and weep (all fees are subject to change, of course):

AIRLINE	FIRST CHECKED BAG	SECOND CHECKED BAG	EACH ADDITIONAL CHECKED BAG	OVERWEIGHT BAG (LB.)	OVERSIZED BAG (LINEAR IN.)
Alaska	Free	$25.00	$100.00–$150.00	51–100: $50.00	63–80: $50.00; 81–115: $75.00
American	$15.00	$25.00	$100.00–$200.00	51–70: $50.00; 71–100: $100.00	63–115: $150.00
Continental	$15.00	$25.00	$50.00	51–70: $50.00	63–115: $100.00
Delta*	$15.00	$25.00	$125.00–$200.00	51–70: $90.00; 71–100: $175.00	63–80: $175.00
Frontier	$15.00**	$25.00	$50.00	51–100: $75.00	63–80: $75.00
JetBlue	Free	$20.00	$75.00	51–70: $50.00; 71–99: $100.00	63–80: $75.00

AIRLINE	FIRST CHECKED BAG	SECOND CHECKED BAG	EACH ADDITIONAL CHECKED BAG	OVERWEIGHT BAG (LB.)	OVERSIZED BAG (LINEAR IN.)
Northwest*	$15.00	$25.00	$125.00–$200.00	51–70: $50.00	63–80: $175.00
Southwest	Free	Free	$25.00–$110.00	51–70: $25.00; 71–100: $50.00	63–80: $50.00
Spirit	$15.00 online, $25.00 at the airport	$25.00	$100.00	51–70: $50.00; 71–99: $100.00	63–79: $100.00; 80–160: $150.00
United	$15.00	$25.00	$125.00–$200.00	71–100: $125.00	63–115: $175.00
US Airways	$15.00	$25.00	$100.00	51–70: $50.00; 71–99: $100.00	63–80: $100.00

*The impending Delta-Northwest merger will create one airline under the name Delta.
**Hunters, the fee for each set of antlers is $100.00.

Now, if you have an extra piece of baggage that goes over both the weight limit (which the airlines have lowered from 70 pounds to 50 pounds) and the size limit in linear inches (length plus width plus depth), watch out. You'll be charged three fees: one for the extra bag, one for going over the size limit, and one for going over the weight limit.

There's got to be a better way. My new philosophy holds that there are two kinds of luggage: carry-on and door-to-door.

Believe it or not, there's actually such a thing as affordable luggage shipping.

Affordable Luggage Shipping

Usually when I recommend that people ship their luggage ahead of time, their response is, "But it's so expensive!"

My answer has always been (and is now even more appropriate, what with the airlines' new baggage fees): How much is your time worth? If you can be practically guaranteed that you won't have to spend time schlepping your bags to the airport and through security and then waiting at the carousel with the rest of the crowd, as well as that your bags will be at your hotel when you arrive, well, isn't the cost worth it?

United Airlines is trying to capitalize on people's reluctance to pay the new baggage fees by partnering with Federal Express (FedEx) to ship your luggage and bulky items like skis and golf clubs—for a fee. Its Door-to-Door Baggage service with overnight delivery costs $149.00 each way for flights of less than 1,000 miles and $179.00 each way for flights of 1,000 or more miles.

My question is, Why would anyone *ever* pay an airline to do what FedEx and United Parcel Service (UPS) already do so efficiently?

This is the perfect example of how doing it yourself can be less expensive. Shipping luggage domestically isn't as expensive as you might think. Sure, FedExing a 40-pound bag for overnight Saturday delivery will set you back a few hundred dollars, but if you plan and pack ahead, sending it by 3-day ground service will save significantly on the cost.

Take a look at these numbers for a 40-pound, medium-sized bag shipped one-way:

SHIPPING SERVICE	LOS ANGELES–NEW YORK	NEW YORK–CHICAGO
Luggage Forward	$159.00 (3 days)	$108.00 (3 days)
Luggage Concierge	$228.44 (3 days); $123.65 (3–6 days, ground)	$162.00 (3 days); $96.38 (3–6 days, ground)
FedEx	$117.90 (3 days, Express Saver)	$69.12 (3 days, Express Saver)
FedEx Ground	$33.45 (4 days)	$18.29 (2 days)
UPS	$119.57 (3 days)	$105.76 (3 days)
UPS Ground	$48.80 (4 days)	$26.68 (2 days)

All days are business days

Tip: if you're really looking to save, you can also ship items via Greyhound and Amtrak. For example, a 40-pound package shipped from Los Angeles to New York on Greyhound PackageXpress will arrive in just under 3 days and cost about $44.00. But with both Greyhound and Amtrak Express Shipping, you have to drop off and pick up your items at the station.

My vote? FedEx Ground wins every time.

▶▶ **Luggage Forward, www.luggageforward.com**

▶▶ **Luggage Concierge, www.luggageconcierge.com**

▶▶ **Federal Express, www.fedex.com**

▶▶ **United Parcel Service, www.ups.com**

▶▶ **Greyhound PackageXpress, www.shipgreyhound.com**

Packing Tips

What's the solution to getting around weight restrictions and extra-bag fees? Pack as lightly as possible. If you can fit everything into one carry-on, great (but don't be that guy who tries to cram a 60-pound suitcase into the overhead bin).

One of my favorite resources for learning techniques for packing light is located at **www.onebag.com.** It offers a packing checklist and tips on how to pack clothes tightly and neatly.

What's the best way to pack your bag? The traditional method of folding clothes on top of one another is no good; you'll wind up with folds in all of your clothes. When you use the backpacker's method of rolling up clothes, you're asking for a suitcase full of wrinkled clothes. The most efficient way to pack without causing wrinkles is a method called *bundle wrapping*. It involves carefully wrapping clothes around a central core object, such as an organizer pouch, with smaller, less easily wrinkled items like shorts and sweaters as the inner layers and more delicate items like suit jackets as the outer wraps.

Other Handy Packing Sites

Packitup.com, created by "packing expert" Anne McAlpin, features the Ultimate Traveler's Checklist, plus packing tips for cruises, Disney trips, and even study abroad.

Don'tForgetYourToothbrush.com includes lists for different types of holidays, such as those involving the beach, winter sports, camping, or cruising. Once you log in and select the type of trip you're taking, it organizes tasks into lists that set out what you need to think about—not just in terms of what to pack, but also related to-dos like stopping your newspaper delivery. These lists are e-mailed to you 2 weeks before, 1 week before, and 1 day before your trip.

The Universal Packing List has a wacky Web address, http://upl.codeq.info, but it cleverly generates a custom packing list based on your activities and the climate at your destination. The site also generates a list of things you need to do before your trip, such as getting the necessary vaccinations, and reminds you of the important documents you'll need.

▶▶ **PackItUp.com,** www.packitup.com

▶▶ **Don't Forget Your Toothbrush,** www.dontforgetyourtoothbrush.com

▶▶ **The Universal Packing List,** http://upl.codeq.info

Compression Packing

Travel-gear companies such as Eagle Creek and Travelon manufacture compression sacks that cost about $8.00 to $25.00 through companies like Magellan's. Essentially a plastic bag for your bulky jackets or dirty clothes, a compression sack reduces the contents' bulk by up to 80 percent once you squeeze out the air.

> **Tip:** How about creating space in your suitcase by skimping on underwear? If you're not one to wash your undergarments in sinks, try packing disposable underwear to use once before throwing it away, creating additional room in your suitcase. Travelingchic.com offers disposable women's underwear for about $4.00 for two pairs. Underworks.com sells disposable men's boxers in sets of six for $8.00, as well as other styles of men's and women's disposable underwear. Or, you can simply head to the closest drug store, buy a pack of cheap underwear, and throw them out after wearing them!

And, If All Else Fails . . .

Wear your suitcase on the plane. This is the ultimate money-saving baggage tip. Sound outrageous? It is, but read on.

There's a wacky new travel-clothing company called **Scottevest/SeV** that proves that necessity really is the mother of invention. The company's travel vests and jackets have between 19 and 52 pockets, which means that *you* are your own carry-on item. You can literally pack an entire suitcase into the pockets of these vests and jackets and wear them on to the plane! They cost—depending on the material and insulation—between $100.00 and $340.00.

Yes, you may end up looking like the Michelin Man, but think of the money and time you'll save. Wear it for just six round-trips and it pays for itself!

▶▶ Scottevest/SeV, www.scottevest.com

Losing Your Luggage

If you still insist on checking bags and the airline loses them, here's how not to lose money when it comes to compensation.

In theory, airlines are liable for up to $3,000.00 for bags lost or damaged on domestic flights. But throughout my entire career, I've never seen anyone get a $3,000.00 check for a lost bag.

Currently, there are two systems in place that cover the liability of international carriage of passengers, baggage, and cargo: the amended Warsaw Convention of 1929 and the Montreal Convention of 1999, which has been ratified in the United States and European Union, among other places.

On international flights (including US portions of international journeys) originating in countries under the Warsaw Convention, airlines are liable for up to $9.07 per pound ($20.00 per kg) for checked baggage and $400.00 per passenger for unchecked baggage.

For international travel (including US portions of those journeys) originating in countries under the Montreal Convention, an airline's maximum liability is 1,000 Special Drawing Rights (based on a mixture of major international currencies), which amounts to about $1,500.00.

However, most airlines' contracts of carriage state that they aren't liable for, well, pretty much anything of value that you check in. Just take a look at Delta's domestic contract of carriage, for example, and you'll see that you check the following items at your own risk:

1. Items Deemed to Be Fragile, Perishable, or Precious
   The classes of items listed below are deemed to be fragile, perishable, precious, or otherwise unsuitable as checked baggage and will not be accepted as baggage, except as set forth in this subsection.

   a) Artistic Items
   b) Electronic and Mechanical Items
   c) Glass: Terrariums, mirrors, crystal, china and glass containers for liquors, wines, beer, liqueurs, and perfumes, and similar items fabricated from glass or similar materials
   d) Infant Items: Fragile items for infant care, including without limitation strollers and car seats
   e) Jewelry or Precious Metals
   f) Musical Instruments And Equipment
   g) Perishable Items
   h) Photographic/Cinematographic Equipment
   i) Precision Items: Microscopes, oscilloscopes, meters, counters, polygraphs, scales, and similar precision equipment
   j) Recreational And Sporting Goods
   k) Toys: Dolls, dollhouses, model trains and airplanes, and similar toys of a fragile nature

l) Valuable or Fragile Papers

m) Other Fragile or Perishable Items: Any item not otherwise listed above which, by its nature or packaging, is subject to damage or spoilage during its carriage as checked baggage, despite exercise by the carrier of ordinary care in its handling.

Translation? If the airline loses or destroys your bag, the most they're liable for is your dirty underwear and toothbrush.

Keep Valuables in Your Carry-On

If your bags are delayed in transit and you have to purchase toiletries and other necessary items, remember to keep your receipts for reimbursement by the airline. Even then there's no guarantee you'll be reimbursed, but without receipts, it will never happen.

Some airlines, like United, phrase their policy very carefully: "United may consider up to 50 percent reimbursement of the necessities purchased, taking into account your ability to use the new items in the future." "May consider"? Thanks, guys.

Protecting Your Luggage

If you can avoid losing your luggage in the first place, that's a lot of money—and hassle—saved.

- Start by cleaning up your bag. Bags with dangling tags, straps, and hooks are just asking to be mangled and destroyed in baggage machines. Also, don't put your name and contact information on just the outside of your suitcase; attach an additional tag to the inside of the bag in case the outside one falls off in transit.
- Take a photo of the inside of your packed suitcase for hard evidence of what items are in there.

- Check in early. If you show up minutes before the flight departs, chances are your bag won't make it on the same plane as you. The same rule applies to connections—never book a connection with less than an hour-long layover.
- When you check in, be sure that the destination city's three-letter airport code on your luggage is correct. If it's just one letter off due to human error, your bag may end up at Atkamba Airport in Papua New Guinea (ABP), instead of Albuquerque, New Mexico (ABQ).
- If you get travel insurance, make sure it includes lost or delayed baggage coverage. Alternatively, check with your credit card company, which may offer additional baggage insurance for a nominal fee.
- Ask for excess valuation insurance. It allows you to declare a higher value for checked luggage at a cost of about $1.00 for each $100.00 in declared value above the $3,000.00 maximum limitation of liability.
- If your luggage is lost, file a claim immediately at the airport. Make sure you get the baggage agent's first and last names and direct phone number.

▽ Additional Resources:

Sports Express (luggage shipping), www.sportsexpress.com

INDEX